The Academic Achievement Challenge

What Really Works in the Classroom?

Jeanne S. Chall

FOREWORD BY MARILYN JAGER ADAMS

gp

THE GUILFORD PRESS
New York   London

To my sister, Shirley

© 2000 Jeanne S. Chall; Foreword © 2002 The Guilford Press
Published by The Guilford Press
A Division of Guilford Publications, Inc.
72 Spring Street, New York, NY 10012
www.guilford.com

Printed in the United States of America

This book is printed on acid-free paper.

Last digit is print number: 9 8 7 6 5

Library of Congress Cataloging-in-Publication Data

Chall, Jeanne Sternlicht, 1921–1999
    The academic achievement challenge : what really works in the
    classroom? / Jeanne S. Chall.
        p.   cm.
    Includes bibliographical references (p.) and index.
    ISBN 1-57230-500-2 (cloth)   ISBN 1-57230-768-4 (pbk.)
    1. School improvement programs.   2. Academic achievement.
3. Teaching.   I. Title.
LB2822.8 .C49   2000
371.3–dc21   99-086150

Foreword

Marilyn Jager Adams

Jeanne S. Chall was fiercely proud of her academic achievements. And well she should have been. Born in Krakau, Poland, she was not brought to the United States until she was eight or nine. Though she was brand new to the country and spoke no English, she was placed in the fourth grade for reasons of her age. Even so, as the youngest of five children, she was in the best position to catch up. And catch up, she did. More, she excelled.

Her brothers and sisters were so proud of her that they all pulled together to support her higher education. She attended The City University of New York, earning her BBA cum laude in 1941. In 1945, after a few years of classroom teaching, she returned to school at The Ohio State University where she earned her AM and PhD degrees under Edgar Dale. She was the only child in her family to graduate from college, and throughout her life she remained openly and lovingly grateful to her brothers and sisters for the sacrifices they had made on her behalf. Partly for that reason she devoted herself, heart, soul, and mind, to improving the education opportunities of others, and especially of poor children.

Although Chall became famous for her work on phonics, it was not phonics that she set out to study. Instead—due, perhaps, to the special challenges of mastering English as a second language—her primary interest was in how to help students conquer the complexities of written text. Across her career, she pursued this issue from two directions. On the one hand, she was concerned with how best to help children acquire the language, vocabulary, and attitudes on which literary appreciation and reflective comprehension depend.

On the other, she returned again and again to the challenge of identifying the factors that make texts more or less difficult to penetrate.

Reading well, Chall believed, must be nurtured, for it is a lot of work. With this in mind, she invested herself in compiling anthologies of great literature for children (1963, 1964, 1994). Her book *Should Textbooks Challenge Students? The Case for Easier or Harder Books* (Chall & Conard, 1991) was written in the same spirit. But Chall also understood that children could improve through practice, only that which they had already begun to learn. Thus, in *Stages of Reading Development* (1983b), she set out a rich, powerful, and developmentally sensitive framework for guiding literacy instruction and assessment from infancy through adulthood. Similarly, *The Reading Crisis: Why Poor Children Fall Behind* (Chall, Jacobs, & Baldwin, 1990) presents a strong, research-based plea for greater emphasis on vocabulary and comprehension in the early grades.

In quest of the other half of the issue, Chall's doctoral thesis and three of her major books (Chall, 1958; Chall & Dale, 1995a, 1995b; Chall, Bissex, Conard, & Harris-Sharples, 1996) were on the puzzle of what makes text difficult. For some years, unfortunately, the educational community looked askance at the notion that the readability of texts could be objectively analyzed. Yet, I am pleased to report that, as the field begins to develop the linguistic and technological sophistication to move beyond tabulating word frequencies and sentence lengths, these books are asserting their proper place in the discipline.

Chall's passion was for literacy, in its truest sense—for its pleasures and treasures and, still more, for the opportunities it affords us to learn and gain from the perspectives and scholarship of other minds and other times—provided we are able. Through her work on phonics she learned the hard way that it is at least as important that we be willing.

Chall's treatise on phonics, *Learning to Read: The Great Debate* (1963), must be regarded as one of the most important books of the century in any field. As she used to tell it, the seeds for this book were planted at an invitational conference at Syracuse University in 1959. The charge to the group was to identify those aspects of reading that were most in need of research, and Chall was assigned to a subcommittee on beginning reading.

In fact, the field of beginning reading had been relatively free of controversy for decades. Endorsed by leading authorities in the universities, classroom materials were dominated by a meaning-first philosophy. The first words to be taught were chosen for level of interest, and children were taught to recognize them holistically, by sight—the "look–say" method. Phonics, meanwhile, was seen as complex and unreliable, an ancillary tool at best. As such, it was taught lightly and late, and children were encouraged to use it to aid word recognition only when context and pictures would not suffice.

Despite all the accord, an irksome fly had recently landed in the ointment. The problem was a book, *Why Johnny Can't Read*, by Rudolf Flesch (1955). The book's essential thesis was that American children were not receiving adequate instruction in phonics. Although Flesch was by no means the first or only person to make this suggestion, he had made it in a way that was exceedingly hard to ignore.

Addressed to the mothers and fathers of America, Flesch's book divides itself into two parts. The first part, written in the clearest and most avuncular of professorial plain talk, explains the nature of phonics and its key importance in helping children learn to read an alphabetic script, such as English. Toward the end of the book, however, Dr. Jekyll becomes Mr. Hyde. The neglect of phonics, he claims, was far from any innocent accident. It was instead the result of a knowing and self-serving conspiracy, wickedly perpetrated on America's children by the experts, the schools, and the textbook publishers. More than 30 weeks on the bestseller list and broadly serialized by the popular press, Flesch's book was a resounding success with the public. Understandably, the educational community was appalled.

In short, the problem facing the Syracuse committee was not just how to refute Flesch's accusations, but how to do so in a way that would reinstate the dignity and authority of the field. The best tactic, Chall reasoned, was through the very sort of scholarship that Flesch had challenged. Having gained support from the Carnegie Commission to undertake this task, her approach was disciplined and thorough. She interviewed the experts and publishers for their goals and suppositions, she methodically analyzed the instructional materials to understand their content and dynamics, and she visited hundreds of classrooms to watch the programs at work. In addition, she assiduously synthesized the extant research literature on the issue—and there was the rub: According to the research, Flesch was right. Phonics instruction mattered. The deeper she dug, the stronger the evidence became. By an overwhelming margin, instructional programs that included explicit, systematic phonics resulted in significantly better word recognition, better spelling, better vocabulary, and better reading comprehension across the primary grades. Moreover, the advantage of systematic phonics was just as great and perhaps greater with children of lower entry abilities or socioeconomic backgrounds as it was with readier and more privileged children. If these findings were contrary to all she had been taught, they were contradictory of those who had taught her and, indeed, the long-reigning and deeply held position of the field at large.

Many years later, when I was given the task of reviewing the research on phonics, Chall told me that if I wrote the truth, I would lose old friends and make new enemies. She warned me that I would never again be fully accepted by my academic colleagues. She was relating her own experience.

Today, after many hundreds more experiments, many thousands more pages, and many millions more dollars worth of work, our scientific efforts to understand beginning reading only strengthen the conclusions that Jeanne Chall had arrived at in *The Great Debate*. Sadly, however, as the evidence in favor of systematic, explicit phonics instruction for beginners increased, so too did the vehemence and nastiness of the backlash. The goal became one of discrediting not just the research, but the integrity and character of those who had conducted it. Chall was treated most shabbily of all.

In this, her final book, she turns from the reading debate to the broader philosophical division that seems to underlie and fuel it: Is the essential responsibility of education one of teaching the basics or of enabling their application and extension? Through page after page of testimony, argument, and evidence, she documents what should not be said, much less so valiantly defended: Public education is responsible for both. If children come to school without the basics, then schools must teach them. For no matter ecifics of the curriculum or the loftiness of its goals, the opity for advanced work is effectively denied unless and until it in children's reach.

To my mind, the most disturbing aspect of this book is the transparently specious rhetoric through which the advocates of child-centered education deny the value of instruction. Yet, Chall does not rebuke them once. She writes instead that "these strong viewpoints were developed and vociferously defended not from malice, but from the best and most noble of intentions—a desire to improve the education of our children" (p. ix). Gradually I came to realize that reproach was nowhere among her interests in writing this book.

One day, sitting across from me at lunch, Chall paused to reflect on that first year that she had spent in an American classroom, so many years before. I can see and hear her almost perfectly. She was vividly recalling her school days, reliving them in sight, sound, and affect. But the voice that was speaking belonged to Chall the adult—the clinician and teacher extraordinaire—as she carefully observed the child in her mind's eye. Was she afraid? Yes, a little. There was so much that was foreign to her. Was it hard? Yes, it was, for there was so very much to learn. The child she saw was so young—as young and soft as the children with whom she now so often worked. Was it wrong to ask so much of her? She paused for a long while, probing deeply, searching for negatives. Then sadly, wearily, she shook her head. No. It was not. Not at the time, and not with hindsight. That child had learned, and it opened the world to her. But she was able to learn only because people taught her. In school.

Chall's purpose in this, her last book, was to make one final plea on behalf of the many, many children who depend on school for their formal education. We must teach them, and teach them well. Their lives depend on it.

> It is common today, as in the past, to look elsewhere than to educational research for an understanding of the literacy problems of low income children and for ways of solving these problems. Currently, cultural and political theories are offered as reasons for the low achievement of poor children and for the lag between mainstream and at-risk children. Although cultural and political explanations may help us understand the broader picture, in the end they must be translated, in practical terms, into what can be done in schools and in homes. Such translations ought to consider the historical findings of educational research—that good teaching improves achievement and thereby can empower all children and especially those at risk. (Chall et al., 1990, p. xi)

Preface

This book asks an old question, namely: How can we advance the learning of elementary and high school students? It is a question that has taken on great urgency today as work and life require ever greater knowledge, skills, and understanding. I attempt to answer this question through an analysis of the literature, relevant research, historical writings, and the writings and observations of teachers, parents, and scholars. I also relied on my fifty years of experience in teaching and in educational research and consulting.

It has been a long journey, and a fascinating one. But it has also been a painful one. It was not pleasant to find, over and over again, strong viewpoints that seemed to become more crystallized and more contentious over the years. And these strong viewpoints were developed and vociferously defended not from malice, but from the best and most noble of intentions—a desire to improve the education of our children.

I have tried to look at the events, thoughts, and research of the past century to determine whether we are now doing the best that we can to improve student achievement, and if not, what we *should* be doing, based on what we *do* know.

This volume could not have been completed without the generosity and support of family, friends, and colleagues. I want to express warm thanks to my sister, Shirley Decker, who listened for many years to my early formulations and encouraged me to continue, and to my colleagues and friends at the Harvard Graduate School of Education, who reacted to my ideas and suggested additional readings and people to consult; these helpful cohorts

include Israel Scheffler, David Riesman, Patricia Graham, Howard
Gardner, Jerome Kagan, Richard Murnane, Nathan Glazer, and
Richard Elmore.

I am especially grateful for the generous help of colleagues and
friends who read an early draft and gave me their candid reactions,
specifically, Arthur Powell, Helen Popp, Emily Marston, Elizabeth
Heron, Nancy Neill, Vicki Jacobs, Gail Kearns, and Ruth Litchfield.

Special thanks go to Rebekah Wolman for her assistance in reviewing the research, to Mary Beth Curtis for her patience and ded-
ication in helping me complete the final draft, and to Sharon
Hibbert for her patience and care in producing the manuscript.

Contents

CHAPTER 1

—◠—

Academic Achievement
An American Dilemma

This book is about the effects of different kinds of education on student academic achievement. In essence, it asks the question, Do certain school practices lead to better learning than others?

During the past several decades widespread discontent with students' academic achievement has been voiced by educators, corporation executives, economists, scientists, and the general public (Walberg, 1997). The nature of the discontent has varied. Most observers assert that students are learning less now than they did in the past. Some, however, assert that learning has not declined—that, in fact, students are doing better than ever on standardized achievement tests (Berliner & Biddle, 1995). Although views vary as to whether there has been a decline in achievement, there is general agreement that student achievement is too low for the demands of an advanced technological society—that more will need to be achieved as work becomes more technical and knowledge-based. There is also a growing consensus that the low academic achievement of minority and poor students needs to be improved greatly (Jencks & Phillips, 1998; Venezky, 1998).

The past several decades have produced a great variety of

broad proposals to raise the academic achievement of elementary and high school students. Some proposals call for greater parent involvement; others seek to implement more school choice through the use of vouchers; still others propose better teacher training and higher teacher salaries, a longer school year and school day, smaller schools and smaller classes, single-sex schools, and school uniforms.

More recently, a growing number of proposals focus on changes in school practices. Growing numbers of educators have proposed national and state tests as a means of encouraging higher standards, grade for grade. At the same time many believe that in order to help students learn, particularly those from low socioeconomic levels, it is best not to pressure them to achieve on grade level.

Generally, the changes proposed for school practices fall into two categories: (1) those that recommend changes in instructional practices and (2) those that recommend changes in students' motivations and in broader aspects of child development (such matters as students' choices of what is being taught and how to improve their self-esteem).

These two kinds of proposals for improving students' learning and academic achievement have been debated, implemented in various forms, and researched for nearly a century in American schools. Is there any evidence that one approach is more effective than the other? This is essentially the question that I propose to answer here.

My interest in this question goes back some forty years. In the mid-1950s, when I was just beginning as a college teacher, *The New York Times* carried a story about a new program designed to improve the academic achievement of poor New York City children. The plan was to take them to museums, to the theater, and to other cultural events in order to improve their motivation for learning, and ultimately their achievement. As with all such stories, I found this one to be enthusiastic and hopeful. And, as with the announcement of other new educational programs, there was an assumption that it would succeed—indeed, that it was already a success. I made a note to look for reports of its progress. To my surprise, there were none. The *Times* had stopped writing about it. After a few years I heard that the expected rise in achievement had not materialized.

Why did the program fail? Why, in fact, was it undertaken to begin with, when the evidence from the relevant research at the time would have raised some serious doubts about its probable success? The relevant research findings suggested then that academic subjects were learned best when specific instruction was given in those subjects (for a review, see Chall & Peterson, 1986). Cultural activities are worthy pursuits in themselves, but their direct influence upon reading, arithmetic, and social studies achievement is questionable. This project, and its failure, alerted me to the possibility that educational innovations, even when adopted with great enthusiasm, may lead to results directly opposite from those hoped for. Yet, why did some new programs succeed and others fail? What was common to the successes and to the failures?

In the early discussions about the merits of a new program, little is usually said about the past relevant research on the issue in relation to the subsequent impact on students' academic achievement levels. This omission is rationalized by claims that it takes several years to get the new procedure right and the teachers properly trained in using it. Instead, the evidence given for preferring the new to the old is usually that the children and teachers love it. And yet, were the relevant published research to be examined, some evidence might be found to support or reject the new program or practice.

What is particularly striking about educational innovations is that most were considered successes long before they were actually sufficiently tried and tested. Seldom were they presented together with a rationale based on educational theory and research. Nor had they been tried first in small pilot studies before being offered as solutions to serious national educational problems.

Why did so many intended reforms, undertaken with so much hope and enthusiasm, fail to fulfill their promise? And why did many result in even lower student achievement levels than those they replaced? Of even greater importance, why were the same reforms proposed again and again, under new labels, with little recognition that they were similar to practices or policies that had failed in the past? (Chall, 1967).

I began to view the new educational programs, and those they were designed to replace, in terms of broad patterns, configurations, or ideal types. Although many of the proposed programs had new labels and presented themselves as unique, one could see similarities among them. It seemed to me that viewing educational programs in terms of broad patterns—as done by anthropologists and sociologists for more than half a century—might prove useful in understanding educational practices and change.

I first became acquainted with this way of viewing different conditions and changes through the seminal work of the anthropologist Ruth Benedict. In her *Patterns of Culture* (1946), which I read as a graduate student in the 1940s, she viewed differences among Native American cultures in North America—differences in their thoughts and behavior as well as the ideas and the standards they have in common—in terms of cultural patterns. She contrasted the Pueblos with other native cultures in North America and found a contrast similar to one described by Nietzsche in his studies of Greek tragedy, in which he discusses different ways an individual arrives at the values of existence—the Dionysian and the Apollonian.

The Dionysian pursues his values of existence through "the annihilation of the ordinary bounds and limits of existence; he seeks to attain in his most valued moments escape from the boundaries imposed upon him by his five senses, to break through into another order of existence" (Benedict, 1946, p. 72). The Apollonian, on the other hand, "keeps to the middle of the road, stays with the known map, and does not meddle with disruptive psychological states" (p. 72).

In *The Lonely Crowd* David Riesman and his associates use a similar approach to describing the nature of and recent changes in the American character, delineating two types—the "inner-directed" and "other-directed." For the inner-directed type of personality, "the source of direction for the individual is 'inner' in the sense that it is implanted early in life by the elders and directed toward generalized but nonetheless inescapably destined goals" (Riesman, Glazer, & Denney, 1955, p. 30).

The other-directed personality, contrarily, is the type of character that "seems to be emerging in very recent years in the upper middle-class of our large cities" (Riesman et al., 1955, p. 34), namely, one whose "contemporaries are the source of direction for the individual—either those known to him or those with whom he is indirectly acquainted, through friends and through the mass media" (p. 37).

More recently, in *Systems of Survival* (1992) Jane Jacobs describes two ideal types, or syndromes, underlying human behavior, namely, the guardian and the commercial. Guardians are the military and police, government ministers and their bureaucracies, legislatures and organized religion, whereas the commercial category encompasses traders and producers of goods. Jacobs goes on to show how these two syndromes (ideal types) tend to develop different economic survival systems as well as different (and contradictory) ethical systems.

As I began to consider whether some educational practices resulted in higher educational achievement, I began to think in terms of patterns, types, and syndromes. Can educational practices, philosophies, and beliefs be classified into broad patterns and types? Do some students learn better when exposed to one pattern or the other?

I thought this was a particularly appropriate time to ask such questions. The number of proposed educational reforms seems to be at an all-time high. And precisely when we need stability, we seem to be investing our hopes in one educational change after another—with little evidence that any one of them will improve student achievement levels. Whether because we have too little supporting evidence or simply fail to use that which we have, we go about debating the merits of one or another practice as though we were in an intellectual vacuum relative to our own past experience.

With so many proposed educational reforms, it seemed to me that a broad view of educational practices and preferences might help us gain a more rational view of the newly proposed practices as well as those they are designed to replace. For example, one can find at least two different practices in the teaching of reading: a natural approach that views reading as a sort of unfolding—similar to learning to speak—and another that views reading as dependent mainly on formalized instruction and practice (Chall, 1992, 1992–1993).

In the teaching of mathematics and science we observe similar phenomena at work. At certain times the "real-life" basis of science and mathematics is emphasized, while at other times the more abstract, systematic aspects are considered central.

Similar differences seem to characterize recent recommendations for curriculum reform in high school and college. Greater student choice and more electives are being challenged by calls for a return to core curricula, with required courses for all students.

Can we distinguish broad differences among educational practices and beliefs in the same way that Benedict's cultural patterns defined differences among Native Americans—or that Riesman used to define the different types of changes that have taken place in the American character—or that Jacobs used to distinguish between those who guard society and those concerned with commerce? Such characterizations are used increasingly to portray corporate life. Within the past several years it has been common to refer to changes in leadership patterns as changes in the *corporate* culture. In education, broad differences between two sets of practices and philosophies have emerged over the past century.

Probably the oldest references are to the distinction between "classic" education and "new" education, also referred to as the traditional, old education versus the new, progressive education. More recently, the terms have become more specific, such as teacher-centered versus student-centered education.

If one considers these educational practices in relation to Benedict's cultural patterns, Riesman's character types, and Jacobs's syndromes, there are some compelling similarities. The teacher-centered educational pattern is more suggestive of Benedict's Apollonian cultural pattern and Riesman's inner-directed character type, while the more student-centered practices more consonant with Benedict's Dionysian culture and Riesman's outer-directed personality type.

A student-centered approach tends to view learning as good in and of itself and as a source of pleasure. If learning is not controlled too much by teachers, schools and parents, it will come naturally to the learner. Student-centered schools, therefore, emphasize joyfulness, rely on the child's natural desire to learn, and emphasize his or her individual needs and interests. Under these conditions, learning is viewed as being as natural as growth and development.

In the ideal student-centered school, the teacher remains in the background, the child's learning mainly arising from natural curiosity and desire to learn. If the teacher teaches too much, that is, too directly, it may inhibit the learner, diminishing curiosity and deflating creativity. Thus, the teacher is advised to be a facilitator, a leader, or a coach—as opposed to one who talks at length in front of the whole room.

As noted earlier, student-centered approaches to instruction fit educational philosophies and practices well known from the past and present. They fit in with John Dewey's progressive, or new, education and with informal schools, as well as with Rousseau's free and open education for Emile. Generally, in these situations, students are perceived as good and eager to learn.

In teacher-centered education, by way of contrast, learning is seen as the responsibility of not just the student but also of the teacher. Students are conceived of as being neither good nor bad. Through education, training, and discipline, students acquire the knowledge, values, and skills that will guide their thoughts and actions in adult life. In teacher-centered approaches to educational instruction, facilitating in and of itself is not enough, and interest alone cannot be relied upon. We learn, according to this view, from those who already know and from the accumulated knowledge of the culture. Not all learning is joyful: to become educated one must be able to deal with the dull but necessary along with the exciting and interesting. But this kind of learning can also bring excitement and joy.

Teacher-centered learning fits the classic view of education, with its emphasis on student knowledge and skills. It was the pattern of most American schools through the nineteenth century, and it is still characteristic of prestigious American private schools, Catholic schools, and European and Asian schools.

The student-centered and teacher-centered educational approaches are ideal types—patterns, configurations, or syndromes. As patterns, or types, they do not necessarily share all the same characteristics in their every manifestation. But, overall, the similarities and differences of the two basic approaches are recognizable. As we will see in Chapter 2, most educational practices tend to fall easily into one or the other instructional category. Progressive education, for example, generally makes a good fit with student-centered learning—with a strong focus on a student-centered curriculum and on individuals' reaching their potential as the goal of education. Classic education, on the other hand, forms a better fit with teacher-centered learning, given its greater concern for the well-planned acquisition of knowledge and skills.

These two educational approaches have over the years come to encapsulate strong and persistent differences of opinion. From the early 1900s on, proposals for a student-centered emphasis have been countered by just as strong views on the benefits of a teacher-centered emphasis. The disagreements continue even today.

To give readers some insight into the deep-seated nature of the disagreements, I present some recent literature contrasting the two approaches and their proponents.

The first media commentary is a story that appeared in *Time* magazine in 1981, entitled "Pricklies vs. Gooeys: Conflicting Theories of Learning in the Wake of Head Start," in which the two educational patterns are contrasted (McGrath, 1981). Proponents of student-centered education are called "Gooeys," and proponents of the teacher-centered are called "Pricklies." McGrath's article captures, with typical *Time* breeziness, some key differences between the two educational patterns—both of which were used in teaching reading in New York City schools during the late 1970s and early 1980s.

McGrath noted that Gooeys believed that learning must adapt to the pace of the individual child, who needs a rich environment and stimulation to learn the words she needs. The Pricklies relied on direct instruction, using phonics and a highly programmed curriculum. They held that for children to learn how to recognize new words, they must sound out letters rather than be dependent on just recognizing familiar words (it should be noted that the Gooeys resemble the whole-language proponents of the 1980s and 1990s and the Pricklies the phonics proponents.)

An evaluation in 1977 indicated that in most of the areas tested—vocabulary, spelling, and grammar—"the Pricklies left the Gooeys in the dust." These findings disappointed the Gooeys, who believed that their method was better, and a later comparison was undertaken in a comparable New York City neighborhood. These latter tests found the Gooeys and Pricklies scoring about the same. The Gooeys further argued that the standard paper-and-pencil achievement tests used for the study were not able to measure the wide-ranging benefits of their more creative approach (McGrath, 1981, p. 107).

As we will see in Chapter 5, these reactions are similar to those found in earlier and later comparisons. When teacher-centered practices "win out," there is usually strong objection from the student-centered camp to the effect that the tests used were inadequate for the broader purposes of education and therefore the children could not show what they really knew. It is also important to note that the Pricklies (teacher-centered students) have been found consistently to have higher reading achievement in the reading research literature from the early 1900s to the present (Chall, 1996a).

An interesting pair of anecdotes in Dina Feitelson's *Facts and Fads in Beginning Reading* (1988) illustrates the wide gap between the two approaches. Feitelson describes two classes of five-year-olds who are learning to swim. In one class, which fits our teacher-centered type, the school's headmistress gave the swimming lessons herself with a number of mothers helping with the dressing and undressing. The headmistress demonstrated the way the children were to walk up the steps facing the pool, turn around on top, and descend the ladder into the pool, backside first. She supervised each child's performance, lending a helpful hand as needed to those who had difficulty. Once inside the pool, the children paired off and faced each other. They had no difficulty moving around and following directions, since the water was only knee high. They were directed in quick succession to jump, stomp, and exchange sides—quickly. Before long they were wet all over. In less than ten minutes, essential first steps in learning to swim, as well as prescribed conduct for safe and hygienic pool use, had been taught, and "initial hesitations and fears had been disposed of before they had a chance to take root" (Feitelson, 1988, p. 38).

In another school, one that seemed to follow student-centered practice, the children undressed in rooms designed for that purpose, then came to the poolside area (Feitelson, 1988). The pool had been fully filled, the water reaching to the children's chest or shoulders. The aim of the initial lesson was to get the children "acquainted" with the water. At all times at least one and sometimes two or more teachers were in the water with the children. No formal instruction was planned. Encouraged by the adults, the children got into the pool, splashing about. A few wet their faces or tried to dive. The adults inside the pool showed appreciation for these efforts and encouraged all the children to join in the activities. From time to time teachers organized a kind of joint activity, such as forming a circle and dancing. Some children just stood around shivering, not participating in any activity. Others refused to stay in the pool at all. Much attention and coaxing were lavished on those who held back, both inside the pool and beside it. The group was in the water for about twenty minutes, and by the time the children and teachers came out, some of them seemed quite cold, with instances of chattery teeth and bluish lips (Feitelson, 1988, p. 38).

Feitelson noted that what especially distinguished these two swimming lessons was

> the way they seemed to exemplify two diametrically different approaches to instructional processes and to the role of the educator. In the first approach it is clearly the teacher who orchestrates the learning experience. Making judicious use of his or her professional expertise, the instructor segments the learning task into a series of steps through which the learner is subsequently led. The crucial point in this approach is that learning tasks are subdivided in such a way that each step can, according to the professional judgment of the instructor, be undertaken by the prospective learners without undue difficulty. . . . (Feitelson, 1998, p. 38)

In the second approach, it is the student who seems to be given the control. The skillful or self-assured students attracted favorable comments, while the reluctant students were made aware of their shortcomings.

My next illustration is from a 1995 article in *Teachers Magazine* in which Ruenzel discusses differences among educational approaches in terms of the traditional/progressive typology.

He begins:

> In the battle for the hearts and minds of America's public schoolchildren, old-line traditionalists and reform-minded progressives are embroiled in a seemingly endless knock-em-down brawl. The traditionalists tend to favor order, strong-headed teachers, and exacting standards. For progressives, on the other hand, learning is like the blooming of a flower. It can never be compelled, only tended by nurturing teachers. (Ruenzel, 1995, p. 23)

The traditional and progressive schools discussed by Ruenzel differed in what the children did, in what the teachers expected— even in how the visitor was greeted. The posters that were displayed also differed. In February, President's Month, the traditional school had dual posters of Washington and Lincoln in the classrooms, while in the reform-minded progressive school, "you'd never know it was President's month, or any month for that matter" (Ruenzel, 1995, pp. 23–34).

The focus of the traditional school was on academics, while in the progressive school the focus was on the joy of learning. Some of the educators who preferred an academic emphasis were concerned that without a grasp of basic skills students would never be capable of meaningful creative expression.

Those who favored progressive education were usually opposed to having students compete among themselves. Consequently, some schools dropped spelling bees and other academic competitions. The report cards in many schools became two- to six-page yearly narratives in which the teacher "reflected" upon the student's personal growth.

> We don't compare John with Sara, we compare John with John. . . . Our teachers will never talk about a kid's relative status. And we don't talk about grade-appropriate levels or abilities either because kids may very well be at different places socially and academically. (Ruenzel, 1995, p. 28)

To meet these objectives, Ruenzel observed, it was essential for the progressive teachers to have an intimate knowledge of each child's interests and needs; they were always creating and customizing learning environments (1995).

The foregoing examples of the two educational types were selected to give the reader a quick overview of their characteristics. As noted earlier, they should be viewed as ideal types that do not necessarily exist in reality. In Chapter 2 I present additional characterizations of these educational types as they are explained by their authors over the period of roughly the past century. What is particularly worthy of note is that, although these types may differ over time, the basic distinction remains largely the same; namely, teacher-centered education is concerned primarily with academic learning, while student-centered education focuses more on student development and motivation.

Do such clear-cut distinctions exist in reality? Some recent historical analyses assert that the distinctions are less clear than previously thought and that progressive education, for example, was practiced only by a comparatively small minority of teachers. Indeed, the practices of most teachers, they claim, could better be viewed as hybrids drawing from both approaches (Cuban, 1993).

Another difficulty in distinguishing between the two basic approaches is the measure used to test differences. If only scores on standardized tests are used, some claim that a teacher-centered approach may have the advantage since its focus on achievement is similar to that of the standardized tests.

To overcome possible biases, I looked at a variety of evidence—historical accounts, descriptive and qualitative observations, reports of teachers and parents, as well as quantitative research. I also examined comparisons between school practices in America, and those in Europe and Asia, and looked for evidence of how much different backgrounds, abilities, and grade placements of students appeared to matter. It is through an appreciation of all these different measures that I sought to find out what educational type is best for academic achievement.

Considerable research has found academic achievement in the early school years to predict later academic achievement. More recently, school achievement has been shown to be related to subsequent work productivity and to income (Murnane & Levy, 1996).

When the scores on standardized tests have been compared with teachers' judgments and other qualitative measures, the correlations have been positive and quite high. For most students, scores on various types of reading achievement tests are quite similar. In turn, these scores correlate well with teachers' judgments (Chall, Bissex, Conard, & Harris-Sharples, 1996).

Academic achievement is also related in part to the ability to function in society generally. Troubled adolescents, unmarried teenaged mothers, and male prisoners have all been found to have lower academic achievement, on average, than their intellectual abilities would predict.

Low academic achievement is a serious social problem, preventing students—particularly in the inner cities and among minority, ethnic, and immigrant groups—from reaching their true intellectual and creative potential. Academic achievement has also become a great concern of American corporations, which increasingly report that they cannot find a sufficiently literate and skilled work force, particularly for the growing "knowledge industry."

In addition to looking at qualitative and quantitative research for answers about the best educational practices for student academic achievement, I also turned to my experience of over fifty years as a teacher, researcher, and consultant.

Chapter 2 describes how various educational reformers and researchers have depicted the trends in traditional and progressive education over the past hundred years.

Chapter 3 presents an overview of the trends in educational policy making as the shift was made toward student-centered programs.

In Chapter 4 I discuss the shifts that have occurred in particular content area curricula, specifically reading, mathematics, science, and social studies.

Chapter 5 presents the quantitative research on the overall effects of teacher-centered versus student-centered approaches to instruction.

Chapter 6 covers the early descriptive studies of such educational experiments as John Dewey's Laboratory School, Bertrand Russell's Beacon Hill School, and the Gary, Indiana, Schools.

In Chapter 7 I am concerned with the links between theories about student-centered learning and the programs that attempt to implement their principles.

Chapter 8 considers the effects of socioeconomic status and type of school (i.e., public, parochial, or private) on students' achievement.

Chapter 9 treats the effects of the home and the community on students' achievement levels.

Finally, in Chapter 10, I present a summary, conclusions, and recommendations.

The Appendix is a review of the key differences between teacher-centered and student-centered educational practices.

CHAPTER 2

Traditional, Teacher-Centered Education versus Progressive, Student-Centered Education

Over the past century, the two basic educational approaches—teacher-centered and student-centered—have been proposed, practiced, and discussed under a variety of labels. This chapter provides an overview of the two approaches by educators, educational researchers, psychologists, and philosophers, and considers how these views became so polarized.

John Dewey used the terms "progressive" and "new education" to contrast his recommended approaches with the traditional, old education. In *The School and Society* (1900), Dewey gives us perhaps the most vivid distinctions between them. He describes his difficulty in finding desks and chairs for his new Laboratory School. After Dewey had questioned numerous dealers at length, one finally understood what he was looking for: "I'm afraid we have not what you want. You want something at which the children may work; these are all for listening." According to Dewey, "simply studying lessons out of a book is only another kind of listening; it marks the dependency of one mind upon another" (Dewey, 1900, p. 31).

Dewey states that this distinction "tells the story of the traditional education"—ugly desks crowded together, as little moving room as possible, and only the educational activities that can possibly go on in such a place, namely, studying lessons out of a book. In traditional schools, Dewey observed, there is little space for the child to work, "create, and actively inquire." In the traditional schoolroom, with its set desks, everything is arranged for handling children in as large numbers as possible instead of as individuals, he also pointed out.

The traditional school seemed to reveal "the uniformity of method and curriculum," said Dewey. "If everything is on a 'listening' basis, you can have uniformity of material and method. The ear, and the book which reflects the ear, constitute the medium which is alike for all" (1900, p. 33). Dewey notes further that there is no opportunity for adjusting to the varying capacities and demands of the students. There is, instead, a "fixed quantity of ready-made results and accomplishments to be acquired by all children alike in a given time" (p. 33).

The key change that Dewey saw coming into education was the shifting of the center of gravity from outside the child to inside the child. In traditional schools, "the center of gravity is outside the child. It is in the teacher, the textbooks, anywhere and everywhere you please except in the immediate instincts and activities of the child himself" (1900, p. 34).

In contrast, within schools that adopt "new education" practices, the life of the child is the all-controlling aim. "The child is already intensely active, and the question of education is the question of taking hold of his activities, of giving them direction" (p. 36).

In *Experience and Education* (1938), Dewey elaborates further on the distinctions between traditional education and progressive education, noting their radical differences in practices. In the traditional school, education consists of imparting certain information and skills reverred in the past to new generations of learners. Thus, the attitude of the pupils must be one of "docility, receptivity, and obedience." Books, especially textbooks, are the main transmitters of the wisdom of the past, and teachers convey this past to the students. "The traditional scheme is, in essence, one of imposition from above and from outside. It imposes adult standards, subject-matter, and methods upon those who are only growing slowly toward maturity" (pp. 2–4).

Despite his enthusiasm for basing new education on experience, Dewey is far from dismissing the importance of knowledge: "No experience is educative that does not tend both to knowledge of more facts and entertaining of more ideas and to a better, a more orderly management of them" (1938, p. 102). He notes further that, when education is based on experience, "the organized subject-matter of the adult and the specialist cannot provide the starting point. Nevertheless, it represents the goal toward which education should continuously move" (p. 103).

He concludes, as he began, with a consideration of the two kinds of education:

> I have used frequently in what precedes the words "progressive" and "new" education. I do not wish to close, however, without recording my firm belief that the fundamental issue is not of new versus old education nor of progressive against traditional education but a question of what anything whatever must be to be worthy of the name *education*. (Dewey, 1938, p. 115)

SILBERMAN'S INFORMAL
VERSUS FORMAL SCHOOLS

Nearly 100 years after Dewey's earliest educational writings, Charles Silberman (*Crisis in the Classroom*, 1970) provided us rich, detailed, and enthusiastic portraits of both an informal English infant school and a traditional school in a work strongly reminiscent of Dewey's contrasting of progressive and traditional schools.

Silberman describes the typical adult reaction to the English informal school as "disorienting," assuming one is accustomed to traditional formal schooling. To begin with, he notes, "the classroom does not *look* like a classroom. It is, rather, a workshop in which 'interest areas' take the place of the familiar rows of desks and chairs and in which individualized learning" takes place (Silberman, 1970, p. 221). To capture the essence of a formal classroom, says Silberman, one would require only a still camera with a wide-angle lens. But for an informal classroom one would need a motion picture camera with sound to capture the motion and activity of the children.

Although Silberman acknowledges that excessive movement and noise in the informal classroom may produce problems of discipline, he argues that the formal classroom produces discipline problems by the "unnatural insistence that children sit silently and motionless . . . [and] the unreasonable expectation that they will all be interested in the same thing at the same moment and for the same length of time" (p. 229). Besides, he adds, "it is not the children who are disruptive, it is the formal classroom that is disruptive—of childhood itself" (Silberman, 1970, p. 229).

Silberman presents additional contrasts between informal and formal schools. He states that most of the teachers in the informal schools that he visited "were not just concerned with giving their students proficiency in the technical skills and mechanics of reading" but were equally interested in the children's use of their proficiency and the pleasure they derived from it (1970, p. 240). He quotes the head of a London Infant School as saying, "If my children get perfect reading scores and then grow up to read only the tabloids and movie magazines, I shall have failed. My job is to develop attitudes and values as well as skills" (p. 240).

Silberman makes still another distinction between formal and informal schools. In informal schools, he notes, children work at their own rate, either on their own or with other children. This approach gives teachers more time and energy to deal with individual instruction. "The openness of the informal classroom, and the fact that children's activities grow out of their own interests, will, it is hoped, sharply reduce the incidence of learning disabilities and behavior problems" (p. 287).

Thus, Silberman calls for informal schools in place of traditional schools as a means of enhancing the child's learning and psychological well-being.

JACKSON'S MIMETIC VERSUS TRANSFORMATIVE EDUCATION

About two decades after Silberman and more than a century after Dewey's earliest works, Philip Jackson presented his "mimetic" and "transformative" educational traditions, which bear a strong resemblance to Dewey's traditional and progressive education, to Silberman's formal and informal education, and to our teacher-centered and student-centered typology.

Jackson suggests in *The Practice of Teaching* (1986) that we think of the mimetic and transformative "not simply as two viewpoints on educational matters but as two traditions within the domain of educational thought and practice" (p. 116). He asserts that "each has a long and respectable history going back at least several hundred years and possibly beyond" (p. 116).

The mimetic, from the Greek *mimesis* (from which we get mime and "mimic"), "gives a central place to the transmission of factual and procedural knowledge from one person to another, through an essentially *imitative* process" (Jackson, 1986, p. 117).

Mimetic knowledge, "identifiable in advance of its transmission," is *second-hand* knowledge, according to Jackson. It has to belong to someone before it can be passed along to someone else. "In short, it is knowledge 'presented' to a learner, rather than 'discovered' by him or her" (Jackson, 1986, p. 117). Mimetic knowledge can be passed either from one person to another or from a text to a person. It is reproducible and can be judged right or wrong.

The transformative tradition, on the other hand, is concerned with traits of character and personality that are valued by the society at large and that are "more deeply integrated and ingrained within the psychological makeup of the student" and therefore, according to Jackson, "more enduring—than are those sought within the mimetic" (Jackson, 1986, p. 121).

The dominant metaphor of the mimetic is one of "adding on" to what already exists (new knowledge, new skills, etc.) rather than modifying the would-be learner in some more fundamental way, as in the transformative. Transformation of "character, morals and virtue" and, more recently, "attitude, values and interest" are usually treated as "more exalted and noble than the more mimetic type of teaching" (Jackson, 1986, p. 121).

Thus, for the mimetic teacher, knowledge may be seen as riches and learners as vessels into which knowledge is poured and stored. The metaphor for the transformative teacher is closer to that of a potter working with clay: the teacher-as-artist, the teacher-as-creator.

It is rare, Jackson notes, to find pure examples of either type, but one type may predominate in certain teaching situations. Methods close to pure mimetic teaching may be found in rudimentary skill instruction, such as the teaching of dancing or typing. And some disciplines are closer to one or the other tradition. Thus, the science teacher, who is principally concerned with the transmission of principles and facts, works mainly within the mimetic tradition, while the humanities teacher is more likely concerned with the transformative tradition. Educators who work with young children seem more naturally drawn toward the transformative tradition than those who work with mature adults.

Toward which of these two educational traditions are we moving? Jackson notes that we seem "to be moving in the direction of becoming increasingly mimetic" and less transformative. "Moreover, I suspect the drift in this direction has been going on for generations, if not centuries" (p. 131). The most obvious signs of this trend, observes Jackson, are that we seem to be gradually turning away from

> transformative goals that over the years have been called character, moral development, deportment, good conduct, and citizenship. . . . Public schools are far less engaged in trying to shape and mould what today might be called the personality of their students than was true a generation or two ago. (Jackson, 1986, p. 131)

Jackson notes further that discussions about schools have shifted from morality and character to discussions of basic skills, competency, and accountability. "That shift in the language of educational goals and purposes is the most clear-cut sign of the move toward the mimetic tradition" (1986, p. 132). Yet another sign of the growing importance of the mimetic, according to Jackson, is the historical link between psychology and education, psychology being, almost from the start, "oriented in the direction of the mimetic tradition within teaching, as it continues to be today" (p. 138). Jackson concludes by noting that there have also been different preferences expressed for the two traditions based on which social classes are being educated, the transformative generally being preferred for elites and the mimetic for the working class and the poor.

INTELLECTUALIST VERSUS
ANTI-INTELLECTUALIST EDUCATION

More recently, Harold Stevenson and James Stigler (1992) have focused on two basic traditions in education, what they call the "intellectualist" and the "anti-intellectualist." Since the end of the nineteenth century, they note, educators have aligned themselves with one or the other of these two basic positions on education. "The first, which the historian Richard Hofstadter terms 'Intellectualist,' defines the goal of education as the mastery of core academic subjects by everyone" (Stevenson & Stigler, 1992, p. 107). The opposing position asserts that the Intellectualist is "old-fashioned" and "unrealistic" in a democratic society that educates children of widely different abilities, backgrounds, and interests. The "anti-intellectualist position" argues that "the goal of education is to meet the needs of individual students, which may or may not include a primary emphasis on academic learning." According to Stevenson and Stigler, "the anti-intellectualist position has gradually dominated the debate, and it remains popular today" (1992, p. 107).

The authors trace the debate over the past century or so, starting with a National Education Association (NEA) report in 1893 (a time when the content of the school curriculum was still highly academic), which proposed that

> every subject which is taught at all in a secondary school should be taught in the same way and to the same extent to every pupil so long as he pursues it, no matter what the probable destination of the pupil may be or at what point his education is to cease. (Stevenson & Stigler, 1992, p. 107)

By the time the NEA issued a similar report, in 1918, the function of the schools was viewed differently. In broad terms that report proposed instead that children need not necessarily meet *all* academic requirements in order to become participating citizens in a democratic society. Rather, schools should be expected to respond differentially to the needs of different children, and the basis of differentiation was to be vocational.

More recently, Patricia Albjerg Graham (1999) observed that

as early as 1947 the U.S. Commission on Life Adjustment Education for Youth, a group of educators, declared that the goal of schooling was to help young people "adjust to life." Graham notes that the commission showed comparatively little concern for "academic matters as a function of schooling, and instead stressed children's nonacademic needs: physical, mental, and emotional health ... [as well as] personal satisfactions and achievements for each individual within the limits of his abilities" (Graham, 1999, p. 44). Thus, given competing views about education's role in improving students' lives—either to help students to adapt to current circumstances, or to assist them in changung those circumstances by learning new knowledge and skills—the commission seemed to favor the former.

Such changes in educational objectives, Stevenson and Stigler note, have had a profound effect on the schools, particularly on the curriculum (1992). The number of new nonacademic course offerings has ballooned, although the absolute number of traditional courses did not fall. The new courses that were created were designed to meet the expanded needs and diverse abilities of a rapidly increasing population.

Stevenson and Stigler note that those advocating the new curriculum held that their approach was "more democratic" and "more fair than the old academic curriculum": "If all children would study in tracks where they could succeed, then each would have the opportunity to enter society with a positive self-image and with skills that could lead to jobs" (1992, p. 108). They further call attention to Richard Hofstadter's view of the new curriculum, reporting that he regarded it as

> a peculiar self-defeating version of democracy [that] somehow made it possible for [new-curriculum proponents] to assert that immature, insecure, nervous, retarded slow learners from poor cultural environments were in no sense inferior to more mature, secure, confident, gifted children from better cultural environments. This verbal genuflection before democracy seems to have enabled them to conceal from themselves that they were, with breathtaking certainty, writing off the majority of the nation's children as being more or less uneducable. (Stevenson & Stigler, 1992, p. 108)

And from such views, according to Stevenson and Stigler, came "tracking" (within-class groupings and other types of differentiating the able from the less able)—even in elementary school.

Which way are we headed—toward an intellectualist or anti-intellectualist future? In contrast to Jackson, Stevenson and Stigler apparently see us moving toward an even more anti-intellectualist position than we are in today.

Aryeh Davidson, Dean of the Davidson School of Education of the Jewish Theological Seminary, recently called to my attention a book entitled *Commandments and Concerns: Jewish Religious Education in Secular Society* (Rosenak, 1987), which is concerned with two basic approaches within Jewish religious education. One may be described as the explicit, with an emphasis on the traditional and historical, the other is the implicit, with a greater emphasis on immediate and individual experience. The extensive explication of these two approaches in Rosenak's volume bears many similarities to our own discussion of teacher-centered and student-centered educational approaches.

THINKING VERSUS KNOWING

A relatively new call for reform comes from those who wish to have schools pay more attention to developing student's practical thinking abilities. They share a common concern for focusing less on facts, knowledge, and rote skills and more on thinking, problem solving, understanding, and creating. The current concern for teaching "thinking skills" resembles in certain respects the progressive education principles of John Dewey and Philip Jackson's transformative education (see pages 15–17, 18–20).

It has also been an acknowledged goal of traditionalists who have been strong critics of progressive education (see the discussion of Mortimer Smith, page 37). It has also been cited as the ultimate objective of education in Alfred North Whitehead's scheme (see pages 31–32). Indeed, both advocates—those for teacher-centered approaches as well as the student-centered initiatives—have been strong proponents of the school's ultimate responsibility to teach basic thinking skills for coping with life and the increasing pace of change.

The current emphasis on the need for a "thinking curriculum" also derives from the phenomenal growth of scientific knowledge, making it impossible for one to learn in school "all that one really needs to know." Therefore students need to be able to learn *how* to think, and to solve problems.

Proponents of the thinking curriculum may differ on when best to start, with one group urging its adoption as early as the primary grades and such traditional proponents as Whitehead and Mortimer Smith advocating a more gradualist pace (i.e., later-grade implementation).

Resnick, Klopfer, and Leopold, in *Toward the Thinking Curriculum* (1989) strongly advocate the teaching of thinking skills right from the start of schooling. They makes an eloquent plea for a curriculum based on thinking, since knowledge in and of itself may be of little use today. What we need today, they argue, is emphasis on the thinking processes, "by which one discovers and validates knowledge. . . . Emphasis should be given to developing these skills using disciplinary and cultural knowledge as a means, not an end, for educating a literate citizenry" (Arthur R. Costa cited in Resnick et al., 1989, pp. vi–vii).

Resnick and associates acknowledge that having students become competent thinkers has long been an educational ideal. But what is different about the new emphasis on thinking is that thinking is not restricted to some advanced or "higher order" stage of mental development. "Instead, 'thinking skills' are intimately involved in successful learning of even elementary levels of reading, mathematics, and other subjects" (1989, p. 1).

Thinking skills, they affirm, must pervade the entire school curriculum for all students, from the earliest grades on. This is so, they note, because to know something is not just to have received information or to know how to perform some action. It means knowing "when to perform it and to adapt the performance to varied circumstances" (pp. 3–4).

Throughout the book Resnick et al. affirm that the thinking curriculum "respects knowledge and expertise" (as does traditional education). Indeed, they note that various studies have shown that "experts on a topic reason more powerfully about that topic and learn new things related to it more easily than they do on other topics." Resnick et al., state that this is true for all fields of expertise, including science, mathematics, political science, and technical skills. "We learn most easily when we already know enough to have organizing schemas that we can use to interpret and elaborate upon new information" (1989, pp. 4–5).

Howard Gardner's "teaching for understanding" (see Gardner & Boix-Mansilla, 1994) takes a similar position, arguing for the growing importance of thinking and understanding skills. But he seems to place even more importance on the traditional academic disciplines as a route to the development of thinking and understanding. He also stresses the developmental aspects of teaching for understanding. He notes, for example, that typically the difference between an eight-year-old and a four-year-old in regard to their ability to think lies in the eight-year-old's potential for "reflecting critically on an answer, for drawing on relevant daily experience, for engaging in discussion and dialogue and benefiting from such interchange" and not so much in greater disciplinary knowledge by the eight-year-old.

> By the middle years of elementary school, most children are ready to adopt some of the habits of the disciplined thinker. As budding scientists, they can think about empirical claims and the evidence that supports or undercuts them; as incipient historians, they can understand the difference between a historical and a fictional account and appreciate the role of records and texts in the creation of a historical account; as aspiring artistic practitioners, they can assume the role of the critic as well as that of the creator. . . . (Gardner & Boix-Mansilla, 1994, p. 206)

At the higher levels, thinking, according to Gardner, requires knowledge of the traditional disciplines. While some general strategies are helpful for thinking, a high level of thinking and problem solving is specific to each of the major disciplines. Thus, Gardner's curriculum for developing understanding has many features that resemble the teacher-centered approach.

While much of the current concern with thinking skills seems to press for the openness of Dewey's progressive and Jackson's transformative education, Gardner's "teaching for understanding" has a strong pull toward the older, traditional teacher-centered education.

LABELS AND CHARACTERISTICS

It is interesting to note that the foregoing contrasting views of education (as well as those presented in Chapter 1) are all concerned with two educational approaches—the older, teacher-centered one and the newer, student-centered one.

In her Inglis Lecture for 1950, Margaret Mead spoke of three images of schools: the little red schoolhouse, the academy, and the city school. The little red schoolhouse, she noted, taught the children pretty much what their parents had learned; new teaching was viewed with suspicion. The academy initiated the children of the privileged into the mysteries of our heritage from Europe, Greece, and Rome. "Both the academy and the little red schoolhouse structured the child's future in terms of the past." By contrast, in the third school type—the city school attended by children of poor immigrants—children are taught,

> not the constancies of their parents' past, as in the little red schoolhouse, or the precious values of a long ancestral past, as in the academy, but they must be taught to reject, and usually to despise, their parents' values. They must learn those things which, to the extent that they make them Americans, will alienate them forever from their parents, making them ancestorless, children of the future, cut off from their past. (Mead, 1964, pp. 10–11)

The contrasts described by Gardner and Boix-Mansilla resemble Mead's, even though they use different labels and focus on somewhat different characteristics.

Dewey distinguished between progressive educational approaches and traditional ones, between the new education and the old education. Philip Jackson used the terms mimetic and transformative to distinguish his two ideal types. Silberman contrasted the informal English Infant Schools with the more formal traditional schools. Stevenson and Stigler focused on "intellectualist" versus "anti-intellectualist" types of teaching. Resnick et al. and Gardner contrasted a "thinking curriculum" with a "traditional knowledge curriculum."

Thus, in all these cases each observer contrasted or distinguished between two ideal educational types: one more classic and formal, and usually emphasizing the acquisition of knowledge; and the second focusing more on the individual learner and on learning beyond its purely intellectual dimensions. These various approaches and terminologies are constant with our teacher-centered and student-centered approaches. In the educational literature one finds still other labels. For the student-centered approaches one finds the labels open education, integrated day plans, Leicestershire models, English Infant School education, individualized approaches, individualized instruction, open informal classes, and the like. For the older, teacher-centered education one finds such labels as explicit teaching, teacher and textbook-centered education, the old education, formal education, and classic education.

I close with a recent contrast used by Larry Cuban, historian and scholar of American education, in *Education Week* (1998). Although he has written widely on the considerable overlap in the practices of old and new education, he now presents a story reminiscent of those cited often in the early part of this century. Contrasting progressive with traditional education, he argues that "good schools" result from both approaches, progressive and traditional, and that the great struggles of the past and present around these two contrasting prototypes have to do with goals more than they do with teaching and learning. Cuban's description of the two types of schools is of special interest to our study, since it is the latest in a long line of such descriptions that started more than a century ago.

Cuban creates a "verbal collage" of two elementary schools he knew. The traditional school is "a quiet, orderly school where the teacher's authority is openly honored by both students and parents" (Cuban, 1998, p. 48). High academic standards are set, as are rules regarding regular school habits. Drill and practice are parts of the lessons, and report cards are sent home regularly. The progressive school, in contrast, prizes freedom for students and teachers. Student-initiated projects are encouraged. There are no spelling bees and no letter or number grades. The teacher describes the personal growth of the student in a "narrative" that is sent home at the end of each year. A classroom banner reads "Children need a place to run! explore! a world to discover" (p. 48).

HOW EDUCATIONAL RESEARCHERS VIEW THE TWO APPROACHES TO EDUCATION

In their various analyses and research reports, educational researchers present rather detailed lists of characteristics of the two educational approaches.

Table 1 presents the key characteristics of the two educational patterns that were widely cited by educational researchers during the 1970s through the early 1990s (see Gage 1978, and Gage & Berliner, 1992).

THE ROLE OF THE TEACHER

Most researchers agree that the teacher's job is more demanding in student-centered classrooms than in teacher-centered ones. According to Gage and Berliner, teaching in student-centered settings "requires constant planning, continuous innovation, a sensitive system of monitoring students' performance, and well-developed skills in maintaining order without being authoritarian" (Gage & Berliner, 1992, p. 486). Maintaining the energy and commitment to accomplish these tasks is difficult even for trained and experienced teachers.

Indeed, even in John Dewey's Laboratory School teachers who followed the new, progressive education were observed to find teaching very challenging. After a few years some left from exhaustion (Hendley, 1986).

A CONSENSUS ON APPROACHES

In general, there seems to be considerable agreement among educators and researchers on what characterizes a classic, teacher-centered approach and what characterizes a modern, student-centered one. There is general agreement that student-centered education has a more integrated curriculum, bases learning more on student interests, prefers small-group and individual instruction, and prefers individual diagnostic evaluation. There is also general agreement that a teacher-centered pattern is more formal, with a curricu-

TABLE 1. Student-Centered Instruction versus Teacher-Centered Instruction

Characteristic	Student-centered schools	Teacher-centered schools
Curriculum	Follow, as much as possible, student interests; integrate materials across subject areas	Standards are established for each grade level; specific subject areas are taught separately
Role of teacher	Teacher as facilitator of learning: provides resources, helps students plan and follow their own interests, and keeps records of learners' activities and use of time	Teacher as leader of class: is responsible for content, leading lessons, recitation, skills, seatwork, and assigning homework
Materials	A rich variety of learning materials, including manipulatives, are used	Teachers work with commercial textbooks
Range of activities	Use of a wide range of activities based on individual interests	Smaller range of activities, largely teacher-prescribed
Grouping and teaching target	Students work in small groups, individually, and/or with teacher guidance based on their own initiative; teaching target is the individual child	The whole class is moved through the same curriculum at roughly the same pace; teacher may occasionally teach small groups, especially for beginning reading, and may provide a degree of individualized instruction; teaching target is the whole class
Movement	Students are permitted to move around freely and cooperate with other learners	Child–child interactions are restricted
Time	The use of time is flexible, often permitting uninterrupted work sessions largely determined by the learners	The day is divided into distinct periods for teaching different subjects
Evaluation	Based on comparisons of learners with themselves rather than with their classmates or grade standards; preference for diagnostic rather than norm-referenced evaluation; deemphasis of formal testing	Norm-referenced tests and grade standards; informal and formal testing
Progression	Learners proceed at different rates	Students are assigned to grades by age

lum divided by grade levels and different subjects, and that textbooks and tests are more widely used in that setting.

In spite of the general consensus with regard to characteristics of each of the approaches, it is well to remember Gage's caution that there is no complete agreement on the importance of each of the characteristics within an educational type. Nor is there agreement even on ways to measure the different characteristics, making comparisons between the two approaches difficult. And yet, in spite of these difficulties, it is important to note the rather strong consistency within each type. And as with other ideal types, it is also important to keep in mind the Riesman and associates' observation in *The Lonely Crowd* (1955) that ideal types do not exist in reality but rather are "a construction, based on a selection of certain historical problems for investigation" (p. 48).

See the Appendix (pages 187–192) for a more extensive characterization of the two educational types as viewed in educational research, in theory, and in practice.

DISTINCTIONS BETWEEN THE TYPES

How distinct are the two types? According to the descriptions presented here and in the Appendix, there is some overlap. Dewey, for example, notes that the new, student-centered education is not opposed to the teaching of facts, knowledge, and skills—strong concerns of the classic, teacher-centered type. Indeed, he writes that education that ignores facts, knowledge, and skills cannot properly be considered education (Dewey, 1938, p. 102).

Philip Jackson (1986) defined his two educational types (mimetic and transformative) reflecting two fundamentally different traditions in education, but he also noted that it is rare to find pure examples of each. However, there is a tendency for one or the other to be predominant in certain teaching situations. As noted earlier, pure mimetic teaching (teacher-centered) predominates in skills instruction and among science teachers (who are generally concerned with the transmission of facts and principles). Teachers of the humanities, on the other hand, usually prefer the transformative or student-centered approach, as do teachers of young children. Jackson also notes that there may be preferences by social class, with the transformative approach usually preferred for the upper social classes and the mimetic for the poor. But there is some difference of opinion on this matter. As will be seen later, the upper class has tended to prefer a more traditional, teacher-centered education, as practiced in prestigious private schools (see especially Arthur Powell, 1996).

Resnick et al. (1989) and, later, Gardner and Boix-Mansilla (1994) acknowledge that a thinking curriculum includes the acquisition of knowledge and skill. They call attention to recent studies that have found creativity and problem solving to be based on a rich and firm knowledge base.

Thus, it would appear that neither pattern stands completely on its own. Those favoring student-centered education make it clear that they do not reject the learning of facts, skills, and knowledge, which are central to a teacher-centered approach. Indeed, they acknowledge that the "basic skills" are the foundation of thinking, problem solving, and creativity. Also, proponents of both approaches agree that the culmination of education is problem solving and creativity (often associated with the student-centered approach).

Indeed, it seems that what is foreground for one group is background for the other. Also, issues of timing may complicate matters further in that many who prefer a student-centered education insist that problem solving and creativity be engaged in from the start, while the proponents of teacher-centered practices usually prefer that the basics be learned first.

THE ROLE OF DEVELOPMENT

A different view of the two approaches was taken by Alfred North Whitehead (Hendley, 1986, Chap. 4), whose formulation was that learning is best accomplished in a rhythmic cycle of stages—from romance to precision to generalization. The stage of romance exists when the individual first becomes aware of the subject matter, with its unexplored connections and possibilities. The stage of precision—the stage of exactness and formulation—follows next, a time for learning grammar, rules, procedures, definitions, and techniques. During the stage of precision the student gains a wealth of facts and a way of analyzing them. But precision should not be an end in itself, but rather should lead to the stage of generalization and abstraction. This, in turn, leads to a new sense of wonder and romance—and so the cycle begins again.

Whitehead believed that education should go through a continuous repetition of such stages. What we must do, he said, is find and tap the unlimited romantic excitement that will motivate the child to acquire the tools of precision that, in turn, will lead to a stage of generalization and a new sense of romantic excitement. The stages are not fixed or distinct, he said, but rather they overlap (Hendley, 1986).

Whitehead later equated the stage of romance with freedom, the stage of precision with discipline, and the stage of generalization with a wider freedom that comes with knowledge and ordered facts. Toward this end he stated that a formal education should allow enough freedom for growth, yet enough discipline for true development.

Whitehead acknowledged that it is difficult to provide discipline and precision without dulling interest, but, he insisted, a "certain ruthless definitiveness is essential in education." The secret is to adopt the right pace: "Get your knowledge quickly, and then use it. If you can use it, you will retain it" (Hendley, 1986, p. 97).

Others have also proposed that educational styles are related to development. Thus, Bloom and Sosniak (1981) analyzed the nature and development of high talent in sports, art, and science and adduced a set of developmental stages. The first is similar to Whitehead's romantic stage, where the child shows interest in acquiring an art or a skill and a parent provides the instruction informally. When the child advances sufficiently, he or she requires a teacher to help him or her become more precise and skillful. At a point of advancing ability the child requires further instruction from a professional teacher who is more demanding of precision and of personal interpretation.

In my work, I proposed six stages for reading development that change as the individual becomes more proficient (Chall, 1983b, 1996b). At the beginning, before formal instruction, learning to read is open and romantic. This stage is followed by a stage of greater precision—learning the relationships between spoken and printed words and between sounds and letters. This is further followed by stages that require more thought and critical reaction to texts.

Many have thus acknowledged that *both* educational approaches are needed for a full, rounded education, where learning is viewed in developmental stages.

Overall, though, most educators have viewed the educational approaches as contrasting positions. This has led to much controversy and disagreement. "Why couldn't one take the best from each pattern?" many have asked. There are many reasons why it is not *easily* done, the strongest perhaps being that the two approaches do represent fundamentally different views on the way to teach and learn. Another is that those who hold these different positions, in their eagerness to explain their own positions, have tended to underplay the position of the other. Thus, student-centered advocates have tended to play down knowledge and skills, not because they thought these unnecessary, but because they claimed that they came naturally from student-centered learning.

Proponents of teacher-centered practices, on the other hand, worry that the basics may be overlooked in a student-centered education. Thus, Lynne Cheney, former chairman of the National Endowment for the Humanities, shows great concern about current math instruction (1997). She notes that the mathematics instruction that has been making its way into schools for several years views mathematics as a natural activity and holds that students will learn only if they are given mathematically rich problems to solve (a student-centered focus). She sympathizes with parents who fear that this idea will prove to be destructive because it does not require that students learn the basic skills of mathematics.

Another reason for the continued controversy and disagreement is that the approaches tend to be presented by their authors and proponents in highly conflicting tones—both a century ago and even more so today. Note the strong contrasts used by John Dewey in his *Experience and Education* (1938) to characterize traditional and progressive education:

> To imposition from above is opposed expression and cultivation of individuality; to external discipline is opposed free activity; to learning from texts and teachers, learning through experience; to

acquisition of isolated skills and techniques by drill, is opposed acquisition of them as means of attaining ends which make direct vital appeal; to preparation for a more or less remote future is opposed making the most of the opportunities of present life; to static aims and materials is opposed acquaintance with a changing world. (1938, pp. 5–6)

Such strong contrasts make it difficult to see "the good" in different approaches.

The tendency of many teachers' colleges to go along with the student-centered approach has also contributed to the "taking of sides." That teacher training was not particularly strong in providing prospective teachers with a broad historical and research view on educational change has also contributed to teachers taking a strong position on one or the other approach.

Still another reason why we seem to have few compromises is the political nature of the two positions. From Dewey on, student-centered education has been associated with a liberal position in politics and teacher-centered education with a more conservative position.

In many ways the two educational types tend to present different world views. The student-centered, progressive pattern has tended to appeal to the romantic in us that seeks freedom from authority and tradition and that looks to new ideas. It is highly optimistic about learning, positing basically that learning is accomplished on one's own, based on one's interests. The teacher-centered view, on the other hand, champions more order and discipline and relies more heavily on past practices for future guidance.

CHAPTER 3

—

Twentieth-Century Trends in Educational Policy
The Shift toward Student-Centered Programs

An overview of the history of American public education in the twentieth century reveals a general movement, until quite recently, away from a classic, teacher-centered approach to a more open, student-centered one. There have been attempts, from time to time, to bring education back to a more teacher-centered focus, but these attempts have been largely unavailing so far. The past several years, however, have witnessed a definite increase of interest in new teacher-centered initiatives.

Some differences relate to the type of school being discussed. Most private and parochial schools have tended to retain their teacher-centered emphasis, but they, too, have moved somewhat to a more student-centered approach over time (Powell, 1996). Also, this general movement in the twentieth century from a classic, teacher-centered to a student-centered emphasis appears to have occurred more commonly in American schools than in European and Asian schools.

Why is this so? The influences are best sought in various layers of our history, economy, and unique experience. Born in rebellion, with a strong belief in individual freedom, we seem to be more open to a greater sense of freedom in the rearing and educating of our children than the older nations.

By the end of the nineteenth century and the beginning of the twentieth, a strong influence on our educational preferences came from our economic growth, as well as the growth and diversity of our population. Our growing economic strength helped to provide us the courage to let go of educational theories and practices followed for hundreds of years in established European countries and to look instead toward educational goals and practices that were essentially new.

The growth of industry and the great number and variety of immigrants raised questions as to how best to prepare all children for a productive life. It appeared to many that the less formal, the less academic, and the more student-centered the education, the more it would suit "all" children.

G. Stanley Hall (1911), for example, called for an education based on the child's natural growth and development. Meanwhile, John Dewey sought to transform the schools and society by focusing on democratic principles, and followers of Freud focused on providing conditions that would foster the student's emotional development.

The educational changes did not come all at once. They came at different times for different social and cultural groups, in different geographical regions, and in different schools. They came earlier in small, private schools with children from economically advantaged families, and later in large, urban schools. Further, while some schools adopted the changes early, others took several decades to do so. Yet, the movement toward student-centered education seemed to affect almost all schools (Cuban, 1993).

Those who favored the new education were not in full agreement with one another. Some wanted schools to pay first attention to the well-being of young children, basing their curriculum and methods on the new scientific evidence on child growth and development. Still others, particularly John Dewey and his followers, had a different focus—one that was primarily social with a major concern for a democratic society. Others sought to emphasize creativity and artistic development. Overall, though, most of those who worked toward the new student-centered education agreed that the first objective of education was to transform, through the schools, both individuals and society—to make both ever more humane, creative, and democratic. Compared to teacher-centered education, the new education was concerned less with academic studies and achievement and more with personal and social growth.

What is perhaps of greatest importance in the change from teacher-centered to student-centered schools was the change in the roles of teachers and students. In the ideal teacher-centered school the teacher is in control; in the ideal student-centered school, the students are in control. Or, as stated by Dewey, "the traditional schema is, in essence, one of imposition from above and from outside" (Dewey, 1938, p. 2).

As with all powerful movements, the new education had growing numbers of enthusiastic supporters and followers. But it also met with strong criticism. Most of the debate was played out between progressives and traditionalists. Among the traditionalists was Mortimer Smith, author of *And Madly Teach: A Layman Looks at Public Education*, published in 1949. Smith objected strongly to the new student-centered education, with its emphasis on educating the whole child and a curriculum based on the child's needs, interests, and abilities. He contrasted these practices with the traditional learning of logically organized subject matter in traditional schools.

A few years later, in 1953, Arthur Bestor's *Educational Wastelands: The Retreat from Learning in Our Public Schools* made an even stronger case against the anti-intellectualism of American student-centered schools, pointedly declaring that "schools exist to teach something, and . . . this something is the power to think" (Bestor, 1985 p. 10). In the preface to the second edition of his book, Bestor charged progressive educators with lowering the aims of American public schools. "And because the sights have been lowered, no possible increase in pedagogical efficiency can ever enable our schools as currently administered to reach the target which the American people originally set up for them" (p. 7).

Noted historian Lawrence Cremin, in his *Transformation of*

the School (1961), placed new education's greatest influence around the 1930s. In *American Education* (1988) he notes that progressive education had become the conventional wisdom in the United States by the late 1940s and 1950s, that it was widely espoused by lay people as well as professionals, and that it was already enshrined in the language used to debate educational policy and practice. In this book Cremin also notes the growth of the progressive movement in Europe and in parts of Asia and Latin America under the influence of the United States immediately following both world wars. This was particularly true in postwar Germany and Japan, where American occupation authorities imposed American versions of progressive schooling.

The changes that took place by the late 1940s were vividly described by Diane Ravitch in *The Troubled Crusade: American Education 1945–1980* (1983):

> By whatever name it was called, modern education by the late 1940s was clearly identified with "functional" teaching, which used everyday situations as the medium of instruction, with the purpose of changing students' attitudes and behavior to conform to social norms. (p. 68)

The ideal, she further noted, was "the well-adjusted student, who was prepared to live effectively as a worker, home member, and a citizen." Generally, the schools were emphasizing "behavior change rather than subject matter acquisition" (Ravitch, 1983, p. 68).

In high school, meanwhile, there was a precipitous drop in enrollment in foreign language classes—from 83 percent of high school students in 1910, to 77 percent in 1915, to 20 percent in 1955 (Ravitch, 1983, p. 68). Changes in high school patterns came fairly early, as ever larger numbers entered and completed high school. Generally the focus for most shifted from a teacher-centered to a student-centered emphasis.

Among other trends suggesting a decline in serious academic studies were certain changes implemented in 1947 on the college entrance tests. These resulted in a change in emphasis from content and the use of essay questions to standardized multiple-choice questions testing verbal and mathematics skills, but largely divorced from specific curriculum requirements.

Negative reactions to progressive education emanated from a variety of sources, Admiral Hyman Rickover (1970) and Robert M. Hutchins (1970), president of the University of Chicago, among them. But there were also positive views, some inspired by trends favoring progressive education in certain Great Society programs and reforms of the Johnson Administration during the mid-1960s.

What was the overall impact of progressive education on school practices? Cremin (1988) notes that the *language* of progressive education probably changed more than the specific ways in which education was practiced. But within the practice of education, small specific, concrete changes tended to be adopted more rapidly than larger, more general ones.

Larry Cuban (1993) found from his various historical studies that in 1916 the dominant teaching practices in most public schools were teacher-centered in terms of furniture arrangement, grouping for instruction, classroom talk, student movement, and work activities. The decades after 1900 saw an increase in efforts to introduce student-centered practices, and by 1940 there was a rapid increase in the "progressive talk" of both teachers and administrators.

Cuban also notes that teachers often compromised between student-centered and teacher-centered practices. In the same classroom, students were seated in rows of bolted-down desks, and the teacher decided what was to be studied and when, what was morally appropriate behavior, and what activities were to occur and in what order. Yet, at the same time, much of the curriculum followed the student-centered model (Cuban, 1993). Goodlad (1983) has also called attention to the fact that, over the years, progressive education has not been as widely (or completely) practiced as many had thought or claimed (1983).

SPUTNIK: A NEW CHALLENGE TO PROGRESSIVE EDUCATION

As noted earlier, there were many criticisms of the new education from its beginning. While it was acknowledged that the results of student-centered education were not always what was hoped for, most educators by the 1950s were confident that, with sufficient understanding and use by teachers and administrators, the new student-centered education would prevail.

It was the Soviet Union's success in launching Sputnik in 1957 that set many to questioning the superiority of the new student-centered education. Fearing that the Soviets, who had held fast to their traditional teacher-centered education, had moved ahead of us in science and technology, there was much rethinking of our student-centered focus, especially regarding math and science. Subsequent reforms in the teaching of math and science during the post-Sputnik years moved us toward a more structured, teacher-centered curriculum that was based more on the nature of what was to be learned—the subject matter—than on the nature of the learners. The overall thrust was to move away from a curriculum based on the learner's interests to a curriculum based on the structure of the discipline. What students were to learn in math and science was planned and organized by mathematicians and scientists—not by the students nor by their teachers.

The new curriculum was planned for and used mainly by the more able students. Somewhat later came a concern for bringing more rigor and higher standards to all students, particularly to those who would not be expected to become mathematicians and scientists.

OPEN EDUCATION

During the 1970s, on the heels of the new teacher-centered emphasis in math and science, came calls for a "new" student-centered education for elementary schools. A pair of articles in *The New Republic* by Featherstone (1971a, 1971b) reported on the new methods of the English Infant Schools that taught young children through adaptation to individual styles. Many American educators soon proposed the same for our children.

It is curious that few noted that the English Infant School's informal education was a later version of methods used by the Dewey Laboratory School, the Bertrand Russell Beacon School of the early 1900s, and other early progressive schools.

Charles Silberman's enthusiastic and highly readable *Crisis in the Classroom* (1970) also brought many U.S. teachers' attention to the wonders of the informal education of the English Infant Schools. The book was very persuasive, and, even before research was undertaken to test these new educational practices, many were adopted with great enthusiasm in the United States.

According to the tenets of informal education, American children were not learning as well as they could because of the "lockstep" education they were receiving in their schools. Informal education proposed, instead, that students be guided to follow their unique interests and to work at their own individual pace. Thus, even before the more demanding, rigorous science and math programs had a chance to prove their worth fully, they were in part countered by one of the strongest of the student-centered movements, namely, informal education. Informal education was also held out as an effective way to improve the acquisition of higher cognitive processes through an intensified focus on student reasoning and creativity.

As with progressive education in the early 1900s, English infant education tended to be favored by educated middle-class parents, while those with more limited education tended to favor a more teacher-centered approach. (Chapter 7 takes up this subject at greater length).

English informal education was one of education's quickest successes—but also one of its quickest failures. Interest in it began to decline only a few years after its enthusiastic adoption (largely because it did not fulfill its promise).

THE DECLINE OF SAT SCORES

The 1970s and 1980s brought additional reasons for discontent. The first was the continuing decline of scores on the Scholastic Achievement Tests (SATs), the decline having begun even as early as the 1960s. Another cause for growing concern was the low achievement particularly among poor and minority children on the National Assessment of Educational Progress [NAEP]. Since 1969, NAEP (also known as "The Nation's Report Card") has conducted periodic assessment of the academic performances of fourth, eighth, and twelfth graders in a range of subjects. At first it was thought that the SAT score decline resulted from growing number of low-income students taking the SAT for the first time. Later, it was found that the absolute decline in scores was even greater among the most able students (Chall, 1989). After years of debate as to whether SAT scores had significantly declined, the College Board changed its standards (permitting a "pass" with lower scores).

Recommendations to improve educational achievement varied widely. Some championed a stronger focus on open education—calling for greater emphasis on student motivation and interest—while others called for more instruction-centered solutions—higher educational standards and greater rigor. The most influential of the many proposals at the time was *A Nation at Risk*, the Report of the National Commission on Excellence in Education (NCEE, 1983). Its proposed solution was largely teacher-centered: a more rigorous curriculum, reintroduction of traditional courses of study, and more-difficult, challenging textbooks.

Other proposals for teacher-centered solutions appeared during the late 1980s and early 1990s. In a series of studies that compared achievement in public schools with that in private and parochial schools, Coleman and Hoffer (1987) found that students in private and parochial schools tested higher on academic achievement than those in public schools. The investigators attributed the differences to the heavier focus of the private and parochial schools on teacher-centered practices such as the use of discipline and assigning homework and grades.

THE SPECIAL CASE OF LOW ACHIEVERS

One of the enduring challenges of the twentieth century has been to determine how best to educate students who find learning especially difficult. Indeed, children who did not achieve up to expectations were among the first to be the subjects of concerted educational research (Morphett & Washburne, 1931).

With the coming of student-centered education in the 1920s, the preferred solution for students who lagged behind was to promote them and to adjust their instruction to their own level of achievement and pace of learning. By the late 1950s it was not uncommon to find students in the primary grades functioning several years below their grade placement—with the gap widening in successive grades. This automatic-promotion policy, now known as "social promotion," has come under strong criticism in the past several years as both the states and the federal government grapple with raising academic standards. Most recently and significantly, President Clinton, in his State of the Union address on January 19, 1999, proposed abolishing social promotion altogether.

The past two decades have seen an increase in special education for the handicapped and those with learning disabilities. There has also been an increase in special programs for those whose native language is not English. These special programs have tended to follow a student-centered approach—oriented to the individual learner and encouraging learning at each student's pace and style.

THE INFLUENCE OF PSYCHOLOGY

An important influence on American education during the past century has been the findings of psychology—its theories and research on how students develop, how they learn, and how they are best taught. Similar to educational theories and practices, psychological approaches have also tended to fall within the two educational patterns—the more formal, teacher-centered and the less formal, student-centered. The psychological theories that were more teacher-centered tend to focus on what students should learn, when they should learn it, and at what level of difficulty. Those that were more student-centered tend to focus on child growth and development, motivation, and interests.

John Dewey's teacher at Johns Hopkins, G. Stanley Hall, expressed a strong student-centered preference:

> The guardians of the young should strive first of all to keep out of nature's way, and to prevent harm, and should merit the proud title of the defenders of the happiness and rights of children. They should feel profoundly that childhood, as it comes fresh from the hand of God, is not corrupt, but illustrates the survival of the most consummate thing in the world; they should be convinced that there is nothing else so worthy of love, reverence, and service as the body and soul of the growing child. (Hall, 1901, cited in Mathews, 1966, p. 24)

This reverence for the child brought Hall to the position that schools should focus primarily on the child's development and happiness, and should relegate academic learning to a role of lesser importance. Indeed, he recommended caution when it came to the learning of reading, writing, and arithmetic. "Before we let the pedagogue loose upon childhood . . . his inroads must overcome the fetishism of the alphabet, of the multiplication table, of grammars, of scales, and of bibliolatry" (Hall, cited in Mathews, 1966, p. 129). To justify making reading and writing secondary to health and happiness, he wrote that "Charlemagne and many other great men of the world could not read or write; . . . scholars have argued that Cornelia, Ophelia, Beatrice, and even the blessed mother of our Lord knew nothing of letters" (p. 129).

Hall cautioned against too much school learning, particularly for the less able: "What shall it profit a child to gain the world of knowledge and lose his own health? Cramming and over-schooling have impaired many a feeble mind, for which as the proverb says, nothing is so dangerous as ideas too large for it" (cited in Mathews, 1966, p. 129).

Much of Hall's psychology was later endorsed by Arnold Gesell and associates, who also sought to explain school learning in terms of growth and development. Their work had a strong influence on the concept of readiness and the value of delaying the teaching of academic subjects until the child reaches an appropriate level of development. If the student was developing slowly, their recommendation usually was to wait for the proper development or readiness before instruction was undertaken (Gesell, Ilg, & Ames, 1956).

The theories of Freud also had a strong influence on student-centered education. Many educational theorists considered Freud among the great educators of modern times, noting that his theories supported the new, progressive education that viewed repression as dangerous to a child's mind. Freud's work helped to promote "freedom methods" of teaching (see Rusk & Scotland, 1979).

Freud's influence was seen particularly in the many new private progressive schools that were established in the early 1900s in the United States and in Europe. Among those in Europe was Alexander S. Neill's Summerhill, which was strongly influenced by psychoanalysis. Neill sought to protect his pupils from the dangers of repression and to encourage them to express themselves freely. He believed firmly that "Human beings are good; they want to be good; they want to love and be loved. Hate and rebellion are only thwarted love and thwarted power" (Neill, 1960, p. 316).

A later influence on student-centered education was Jean Piaget's (1970) work on cognitive development, particularly his conceptualization of the stages through which the child travels—from the sensory–motor (birth to two years), to the preconceptual (two to four or five years), the intuitive (four or five to seven years), the concrete operational (seven to eleven years), and the formal operational (eleven to sixteen years). This growth of cognitive power, according to Piaget, stems mainly from the development of the ability to symbolize. And the force for this development comes mainly from the child—from his or her readiness—not from school learning. Piaget made few references to the influence of parents or teachers in stimulating the child's cognitive development, concluding in effect that the foundation of cognitive growth is in the child's own activities rather than in instruction.

During the 1970s the major attention generated by educational psychology moved from Piaget to Vygotsky, whose developmental theory had much in common with Piaget's but put a stronger emphasis on the importance of learning and social and environmental factors. Thus, said Vygotsky, the development of the mind is influenced not only by biological development but also by society. Vygotsky brought psychologists back to thinking about optimal environmental conditions for learning, including the teacher's role through the provision of supports ("scaffolding"), as well as the appropriate level of difficulty ("zone of proximal development")—the level at which the student can learn with the aid of a teacher or more knowledgeable peers (Vygotsky, 1962). This was quite different from the ways in which Piaget's teachings had been interpreted—that is, as reinforcing teaching to the child's present cognitive development, not to a higher level. The concern of Vygotsky for environmental influences brought back to psychology the more traditional concerns of what to teach, when, and at what level of difficulty.

Education from the early 1900s onward was influenced also by American psychologists concerned primarily with learning and instruction. E. L. Thorndike was the preeminent American psychologist in this group, making significant contributions to theories of learning, intelligence, language, aptitude, achievement, and testing. He also worked directly on the psychology of school subjects—on how best to teach reading and writing to students of different ages and abilities, as well as how to conceive the nature of reading comprehension.

Somewhat later B. F. Skinner focused on optimal practice for effective learning. This led to his work on programmed learning—a procedure by which students learn at their own pace by using materials organized in small, incremental steps. This did not mean that some students did not learn more holistically. But for most, Skinner proposed that learning in small incremental steps was most effective—especially for the learning of basics. According to Skinner, the major focus of instruction should be on the ordering of what is to be learned and practiced.

As can be seen from the foregoing, American psychologists during the past century have had differing views on education, some leaning more toward a student-centered education, others toward a more teacher-centered education. Was one position more influential than the other?

The educational historian Ellen Lagemann poses that question (1989). Lagemann compares the ideas and methods of E. L. Thorndike with those of John Dewey, and asks who won—Dewey or Thorndike? Was it Dewey's philosophy of transforming schools and society? Or was it Thorndike's scientific emphasis on learning and teaching? She notes that Dewey hoped to find in education a scientific method for philosophy, while Thorndike hoped to develop a science of education. Whereas Dewey sought to "change society through educational reform," Thorndike sought to "change education through professionalization" (Lagemann, 1989, p. 205). Dewey saw the school as a laboratory for education. Thorndike saw it as a place for implementing the findings of laboratory research. Another difference was that Dewey saw "...teachers and researchers as more alike than different, wanting both to be skilled students of education," while Thorndike believed that, teachers and researchers should fulfill distinctly different functions: Teachers should teach—"organizing classrooms, and approaching children using the knowledge generated by researchers" (Lagemann, 1989, p. 205).

Thorndike was deeply committed to experimentation in psychology and education and was also concerned with "elaborating a distinctive body of knowledge that would be accepted as 'the science of education'" (Lagemann, 1989, p. 212). He was not interested in the naturalistic participant–observer studies that Dewey carried out during his years as director of the Chicago Laboratory School. Thorndike produced school surveys, curricula, tests, and laws of learning that offered the kind of educational science that many educators needed to explain their practices and policies. He was not concerned with "the significance of education as a means to a social renewal and social change," but saw it as "a technique for matching individuals to existing social and economic roles" (Lagemann, 1989, p. 212).

So, who won? Lagemann's choice is Thorndike: "one cannot understand the history of education in the United States during the twentieth century unless one realizes that Edward L. Thorndike won and John Dewey lost" (1989, p. 185).

It is hard to disagree with Lagemann. Thorndike did win in moving education toward greater use of quantitative research, surveys, scientific experiments, and objective assessment. Yet, I find it difficult to agree that Dewey lost. In spite of setbacks and disagreements, his ideas have endured. Although he goes out of favor for a while, he seems to come back, often under different labels. The current questioning of quantitative research methods and the growing interest in case studies, portfolios, and other qualitative assessments indicates that Dewey's methods of analysis are back today, perhaps stronger than ever.

Also, can we say that Thorndike won when educational practice has had such a long history of not only ignoring its own educational research findings but also going against them? Educators have made use of the scientific efforts of Thorndike and his followers—their work on achievement and aptitude tests, their instructional materials, and their emphasis on education as a profession—but these have become rather routine. Thorndike may remain the psychologist's psychologist; but Dewey seems to remain the teacher's psychologist.

Many of the dilemmas we face today stem from the differences between these two traditions in psychology and education, that is, the scientific approach of Thorndike and the search for social change of Dewey. And, as in the early 1900s, the followers of each approach still tend to oppose or to pay little attention to the other.

Therefore, I think that Dewey cannot be considered the loser. For many educational practitioners he is still the winner. And he is becoming the winner for a growing number of educational researchers who propose moving away from the objective methods of Thorndike to the naturalistic participant–observer type of inquiry of Dewey when he was at the Chicago Laboratory School.

That Dewey may not be the loser can be seen also in some of the current shifts in educational practice—shifts seldom based on the results of educational research. More often they come from broad philosophical ideas and preferences. Note, for example, the popularity of the whole language method in the teaching of reading and writing, a progressive approach to literacy. In the 1980s and early 1990s the proponents of the whole-language approach rejected the accumulated quantitative research on beginning reading that had been conducted from the early 1900s onward. They accepted, instead, an approach that can be better classified as student-centered (see pp.). The present call for reinstating the teaching of skills, particularly phonics, is based not on a reconsideration of the old and new research evidence, but on the disastrous drop in reading achievement in California, a strong proponent and early user of whole language.

Overall, it would appear that the influence of Dewey's progressive ideas on teaching has been as great as the scientific tradition of E. L. Thorndike. Thorndike may have given education the words, but Dewey has given it the music. Dewey's appeal to teachers has been on the broader philosophical aspects of education, and his ideas have been accepted by many almost as a religion.

The two styles of psychology—Dewey's and Thorndike's—differed also on the training of teachers and researchers. The position of Thorndike was that educational researchers were to have Ph.D.s and were to do the educational research that was to be applied by the teachers. The teachers did not need to have Ph.D.s. Their main responsibilities were to teach. Thorndike seems to have won on the issue of teacher preparation. Teachers and researchers are trained differently. Teachers have little exposure to research, and researchers have little exposure to practice. Even today, although most teachers have master's degrees, there is a tendency not to involve them when decisions are made on educational policy. On the numerous policy committees on which I have served, most members were researchers or college faculty. Few, if any, were classroom teachers or administrators. Without teachers and administrators, it is easy to lose a sense of reality. The separation of researchers from practitioners has made it difficult, also, to anticipate whether new practices suggested by research have a chance of succeeding.

In spite of the differences in the two psychological views on education, it is important to note the importance of psychology in the formulation of the ideas of American education. From the early 1900s onward, education has followed the lead of psychology in its great concern for the learner—his abilities, interests, and motivations. There was less concern with the content of what students learn. This orientation can be clearly seen in the preparation of teachers, which typically involves numerous courses in psychology, sociology, and anthropology. (See Chapter 4 for a more detailed account of twentieth-century changes in the teaching of reading, math, science, and social studies.)

PENDULUM SWINGS OR STEADY DEVELOPMENT?

Do the historical changes in American education fit a model of pendulum swings? Or do they fit a model of long-term development? Tyack and Cuban, in *Tinkering toward Utopia: A Century of Public School Reform*, note that "two apparently contradictory notions about schools have persisted side by side over decades"—the idea of steady educational evolution and the idea that educational reforms have come in cycles (1995, p. 40).

They find the idea plausible that most major trends are gradual "and more or less linear in evolution," not fitful bursts ultimately reducible to cyclical patterns. And yet, certain calls for change have occurred again and again in a cyclical fashion and sometimes at a dizzying pace. "Reformers, for example, have alternately proposed student-centered pedagogy or teacher-centered instruction, attention to academics or to practical knowledge, and centralized or decentralized governance of schools" (Tyack & Cuban, 1995, p. 41).

In this section I attempt to show that the major changes in the past century have come about more from steady development than from pendulum swings. This observation seems true for broad issues, nationally. It is quite possible to have pendulum swings in particular schools or districts as they try to meet the changes suggested by national trends.

Overall, most private and parochial schools have changed little during the past century from their teacher-centered emphasis. The public schools, however, tended to move quite steadily from a teacher-centered to a student-centered emphasis in the curriculum areas. In a few areas, such as reading, the move from one to another emphasis seems to have been more cyclical. Yet, over the long haul there is considerable evidence that the changes have followed a pattern of slow development. Irrespective of what it is called, the emphasis in reading from the early 1900s to the early 1990s has been student-centered. The current concerns with low test scores have brought a renewed interest in teacher-centered reading programs.

Reaction to the recent trend toward a teacher-centered pattern is illustrated by the following: A principal of an inner-city high school in New York raised student achievement levels by requiring that students take traditional academic courses in math, science, and English in place of the less demanding ones they had been taking. The plan was succeeding. Achievement and SAT scores were rising and the students were enthusiastic about their studies.

Yet, the principal's plan was opposed by many of his colleagues. They feared that the students were being frustrated—that the more-difficult traditional courses were pushing them too far. Even though the rise in SAT and achievement scores supported the principal's plan, it was not appreciated by his colleagues, who held strong student-centered views.

Changes in Textbook Difficulty

Historical analyses of textbooks show a steady decline in difficulty from the 1920s to the present. The first decline in difficulty was in the reading textbooks for the primary grades. The authors and publishers who were first to simplify the primary reading textbooks claimed that the easier books were more suitable for most children, according to research on their vocabulary knowledge (Chall, 1958). The move toward ease was prompted, also, by the change in methods of teaching beginners to a whole-word, sight method from a stronger phonics emphasis. This change made it harder for the children to recognize new words. Hence, the number of new words to be learned in the reading textbooks was lowered. The easier books were soon considered the better books, and, probably because of competition among publishers, the new editions of the primary readers had fewer different words—that is, they were easier than the earlier editions.

By the late 1930s, however, most of the readers had fewer words than the research evidence indicated was optimal (Chall, 1958). Even so, the readers kept getting easier until about the 1960s when some started appearing to get somewhat harder again (Chall, 1958, 1983a).

Subject matter textbooks also became easier from about the 1940s to the 1970s. In a study commissioned by the Advisory Panel on the SAT Score Decline (Chall, Conard, & Harris, 1977), the most widely used textbooks (readers, grammars, composition and history books) published from the 1940s to the 1970s for grades 1, 6, and 11 were found to be increasingly less challenging. When the difficulty of the textbooks was compared to the SAT scores of students who had used them, compelling evidence was found that those students who had used the more difficult textbooks had the higher SAT scores. This was particularly so for the early reading textbooks. The students who had learned from the harder school readers had higher SAT scores, while those who received instruction from easier readers scored lower.

The decline in textbook difficulty was considerable by the 1970s. The social studies textbooks for the twelfth grade, for example, were written at a level appropriate for ninth graders (Chall et al., 1977). Overall, whether the measures of difficulty used were based on cognitive difficulty, readability, abstractness, or concreteness of the topic, they indicated a decrease in challenge over time.

An update of our study of text difficulty (Chall & Conard, 1991) found no change in difficulty from the 1970s to 1991. Thus, in spite of the calls for more-difficult textbooks (see also *A Nation at Risk*, [NCEE, 1983]) and after conferences (several sponsored by educational publishers), articles, books, and newspaper stories calling for different textbooks, still they did not seem to change (Chall & Conard, 1991, p. 5).

Our findings on the declining difficulty of textbooks have since been confirmed by Hayes, Wolfer and Wolfe (1993), who analyzed a larger sample of textbooks and used more stringent estimates of difficulty. Their analysis of 800 elementary, middle, and high school books published between 1919 and 1991 found a pervasive decline in the difficulty of the books analyzed. When they linked the difficulty of the textbooks to SAT verbal scores, they also found higher SAT scores when more difficult texts had been used and lower scores when easier texts had been used. As with the Chall et al. studies (1977) and Chall and Conrad (1991), they viewed text simplification as signaling a decline in challenge, which in turn led to a decline in achievement: "Long-term exposure to simpler texts may induce a cumulating deficit on the breadth and depth of domain-specific knowledge, lowering reading comprehension and verbal achievement" (Hayes et al., 1993, p. 489).

Changes in High School Course Enrollment

The steady decline of textbook difficulty closely parallels the steady decline in the difficulty of courses of study in high schools from the 1920s to perhaps the 1970s. However, there appears to have been a reversal of this trend during the past decade. According to Angus and Mirel (1995), more high school students have been taking rigorous academic courses, and even the "watered-down" courses have been getting more difficult for about the past fifteen years.

Angus and Mirel's 1995 analysis of high school course enrollments from the early 1900s found "one long pendulum swing toward non-academic subjects that continued for four decades" (p. 302). Their data revealed a steady drop in academic subject enrollments beginning in 1928 and continuing until at least 1961. This drop included a "sharp decline in the study of foreign languages and more modest declines in mathematics and science" (p. 302).

They note further that the data do not reveal the full extent of the changes toward ease, such as the reorganization of English courses into "literature and life" and the increase in offerings of less challenging levels of mathematics and science courses. Overall, though, they note, "it is quite clear that the proportion of the high school curriculum claimed by the academic subjects, whether measured by course enrollments or credits, declined significantly from the late 1920s until sometime in the late 1960s or early 1970s" (Angus & Mirel, 1995, p. 309).

What accounted for the decline in the study of academic subjects? Angus and Mirel explain it as "a slow working out in practice" of the modern educational philosophy that high schools should provide a needs-based functional curriculum (a student-centered emphasis) in opposition to an earlier, traditional teacher-centered emphasis that favored a liberal arts education for all. Even Sputnik had little effect on the courses taken by most high school students. The new, harder science courses were taken only by the able and talented. Rather than searching for new and more effective ways to teach the less able students academic subjects, educators elected to "shunt" these students to less challenging courses. "This belief shaped the direction of most high school curriculum reform after the 1930s and undergirded the life adjustment movement" (Angus & Mirel, 1995, pp. 305–306).

This trend reveals that the new education was far less concerned with academic achievement than with the total well-being of the student. If there was any possibility that the student might fail a difficult subject, it was to be avoided to save him or her from failure and frustration. Modern education sought to make a high school education available to every youth, including those with low achievement. Thus, lower level and remedial courses were offered to one segment of the student population while advanced and college-level courses were offered to another segment. Many different elective courses were offered to meet the abilities and interests of all students, and graduation requirements were relaxed (Angus & Mirel, 1995).

Overall, this trend in high school course enrollment lasted about five decades—from the 1920s to the 1970s—a period of time that can hardly be considered a pendulum swing.

A similar trend can be found in the elementary grades, where some students were taught at levels that were quite low in order to prevent possible failure and frustration. The writings of Dewey (1900), Hall (1901), and Huey (1908) assured teachers and administrators that it was not essential for the child to learn to read until about age eight. There were many more important educational activities for the early school years, such as thinking and solving problems.

That reading was not of first importance in the early years of schooling was accepted by many private progressive schools from the early 1920s until about the 1950s. This view gradually became the policy for public schools, even those with low-income and immigrant children. This was an unfortunate decision, since subsequent research has consistently found that an early start in learning to read is beneficial for most children. Since reading achievement is cumulative, with proficiency in later grades built on proficiency in the earlier grades, a delay in instruction can be significant (Chall, 1958, 1967; Chall, Jacobs, & Baldwin, 1990).

One may ask how it is that student enrollment in difficult courses has increased within the most recent decade while textbook difficulty remains about the same as it was several decades ago. On the surface, raising the difficulty of textbooks would seem to be simpler than raising the difficulty level of courses. However, on further examination one realizes that much more is at stake in raising the difficulty levels of textbooks. The level of difficulty of courses of study depends on the decisions of teachers and administrators. The difficulty level of textbooks, on the other hand, is determined by authors and publishers, and textbook adoption committees, in addition to teachers and administrators. Even more important, perhaps, is that the ultimate decision on textbook difficulty is based not only on educational needs but also on market considerations. Unless publishers can anticipate that more difficult textbooks will be accepted by teachers and administrators, they cannot afford to produce them. And many teachers and administrators seem to prefer less challenging books. They seem to hold on to the concept of minimizing student frustration and failure. Those who teach students who function below grade level fear that raising the difficulty levels of textbooks may hurt most those students who are already finding their textbooks too difficult.

This is a particular concern of teachers of students who have difficulty learning. We saw this at the beginning of every year in the Harvard Reading Laboratory. After administering and analyzing diagnostic tests that suggested optimal levels of textbook difficulty to use for instruction, most of the teachers in the laboratory selected books about a year below the student's tested level. Why, we asked, did they use a book that was easier than was indicated by the diagnosis? Because they did not want to frustrate their student! Thus, it would appear that raising the difficulty levels of textbooks may prove to be harder than originally anticipated.

During the past hundred years, American educational practices moved steadily from a teacher- to a student-centered emphasis. The extent of the changes was not always evident, because there were differences in the changes in the different content areas. For example, reading seemed to change earlier and more clearly than math, science, and social studies. There were also differences in the changes by types of schools, with fewer changes in private and parochial schools than in public schools. Although there is general acceptance that the schools tended to move toward a student-centered emphasis, the exact extent to which changes were actually put into practice has been questioned. Several historians have noted that the actual practices of student-centered programs were more teacher-centered than first claimed or recognized. Recent trends in the late 1990s show a growing interest in a return to the older, teacher-centered emphasis.

This view is discussed more fully in later chapters that will also take up changes in the late 1990s that seem to show, in most subject areas, a return to a teacher-centered emphasis (see especially Chapter 4).

CHAPTER 4

~

Trends in Reading, Mathematics, Science, and Social Studies, 1900 to the 1990s

In this chapter I look at reading, math, science, and social studies instruction and ask which approach was dominant during which period of time and whether the trends identified were supported by research findings.

In the past hundred years there has been a great deal of research on reading and an increasing amount of research in mathematics, science, and social studies. But the research in the other curriculum areas has not been as extensive as in reading. Reading has been the most researched of the school subjects and has been widely correlated with achievement in the other school subjects. It is often used as an index of overall achievement. This practice is easily justified by the high correlation of reading achievement with other academic subjects (Walberg, 1997).

The trends in reading are presented first, followed by those in math, science, and social studies. The reading trends are based on my various analyses found in *Learning to Read: The Great Debate* (1967, 1983, 1996) and my other reviews (Chall, 1987, 1989, 1992–1993); other important contributors to this trend analysis include Adams (1990), Perfetti (1985), Feitelson (1988), and Snow, Burns, and Griffin (1998). The trends observed in mathematics, science, and social studies are drawn largely from reviews in the research literature in three editions of the *Encyclopedia of Educational Research* (Alken, 1992; Mitzel, 1982; Monroe, 1950).

TRENDS IN READING INSTRUCTION

During the past 100 years, reading instruction in the United States has evolved from a formal teacher-centered methodology to a more informal student-centered orientation. Teacher-centered approaches to reading instruction have tended to be formal, utilizing direct instruction from the teacher, systematic instruction in phonics, the use of reading texts that have "controlled" vocabularies, as well as assigned literature and nonfiction.

Student-centered reading approaches have tended to treat reading instruction more informally, relying more on students' choice of the reading materials, preference for children's literature for beginning reading instead of textbooks, and teaching phonics incidentally, "as needed," if at all (Chall, 1992–1993).

The teaching of reading has been the subject of intense controversy for nearly a century (see *Learning to Read: The Great Debate* [Chall, 1967], and the second and third editions [Chall, 1983a, 1996a]). Since the 1920s there have been debates on whether teaching the recognition of whole words is better than teaching phonics, whether the alphabet should be taught before or after words are taught, and whether the child's first reading material should be stories dictated by the children, children's literature, or selections in primers and readers (Chall, 1967).

The current debates, as will be seen later, are quite similar to the ones in the 1920s, with one important difference. The professional literature of the 1920s and 1930s appears to be more reasoned than that of the 1980s and 1990s—an ironic twist, since there is infinitely more published research in the 1980s and 1990s on which to base one's opinions. The literature on reading in the 1980s and 1990s tends to use strong rhetoric, and proponents seem often to base their positions more on ideology than on the available scientific and theoretical literature. The strong rhetoric of the 1980s and 1990s has led many to characterize the ongoing debate as the "reading wars."

For many, whole language has taken on a broader meaning— giving teachers license, some claim, to teach reading as they think best. For others, it simply means integrating the teaching of reading with writing, speaking, and listening. And for still others, it stands for a philosophy of education and of life, not merely a method of teaching reading.

There is a further problem in evaluating whole language, namely, the tendency of its proponents to claim newness for many of its good practices when history tells us they have been in wide use for a long time. For example, many whole-language proponents claim that the use of "authentic" literature is a unique feature of their program. Yet, good literature has been a part of reading instruction since Noah Webster's spelling book. Although whole language proponents tend to blame phonics instruction on a paucity of literature in reading textbooks, one should note that the amount and quality of literature in the reading textbooks usually increases as the teaching of phonics increases. The faster pace of learning to recognize words when phonics is taught makes possible earlier reading of more advanced quality literature. Further, the combined use of reading, writing, language, and speaking claimed by many whole-language enthusiasts as their discovery has been the basis of remedial instruction since the early 1920s, when it was called a multisensory approach.

For this analysis I will consider whole language as a student-centered approach that differs from a more traditional teacher-centered approach that includes systematic teaching of phonics and other skills.

I will discuss, first, the whole-language/phonics issue by considering the reading research and theory of the past 100 years, the applications of this research, and the accompanying rhetoric. Second, I will consider the effects of whole language and phonics on reading achievement, that is whether higher or lower reading

scores resulted from a particular approach (and the related concep-
tions of reading). My main question is whether changes in instructional methodology help to explain the reading scores found in
such large-scale studies as the National Assessment of Educational
Progress, which first assessed reading in 1971, and continues to do
so every four years.

Whole language, although it is considered a relatively new
approach, has deep roots in the past. It very much resembles
practices that began in the 1920s in the early grades, although
those relied more on informal, individualized instruction using
the child's own stories for reading in place of selections in textbooks. Back then, too, the child was expected to infer the specific letter–sound relationships. Systematic teaching of letter–
sound relationships (phonics) was not the preferred procedure.
Instead, emphasis was placed on learning to recognize whole
words (sight recognition) and even sentences. As is true of
whole-language proponents today, the proponents of this method
claimed that the best route to word recognition and decoding
was through reading for meaning right from the start—whether it
be words, sentences, or stories.

Also widely used from the 1920s through the 1960s were reading textbooks (basal readers) that, as with whole language, relied
on meaningful reading from the start through sight recognition of
words. Phonics was taught, but not explicitly or systematically. Vocabulary control was the major way by which difficulty was gradually increased. Although the teaching procedures of the basal readers were more formal than those of whole language, the theory of
reading that both follow is similar—that reading, right from the
start, is basically getting the meaning of text. The more traditional
approaches to reading, those used prior to the 1920s, put the first
task of learning to read on learning the alphabetic principle, that is,
the relationships between letters and sounds.

From about 1920 to the late 1960s, the predominant view on
beginning reading was that language and cognition were the most
important components of reading. From the late 1960s through the
early 1980s, there was a return, for a brief time, to the more traditional conception of beginning reading—that a knowledge of letter–sound associations was most central to beginning reading, and
that this made possible a recognition of more and more words, and

an understanding of text. Indeed, as we will see later, the research from which this concept came has been confirmed and reconfirmed over some eighty years.

The importance of a knowledge of letter–sound relationships has been confirmed by research on phonemic awareness (Rath, 1990). Basing their work on theories of psycholinguistics, cognition, child development, and learning disabilities, many researchers have focused on the centrality of phonology (phonics, decoding, word analysis) in reading development (Stanovich, 1991). If phonics is not learned early, phonological factors may indeed interfere with the use of language and reasoning in reading development. For older students with reading problems, language and cognitive difficulties are not always the central factor; rather, the difficulty may still be mainly with phonics, which leads to further difficulty with fluency and comprehension. Research on very young children has confirmed findings from the 1930s that phonological awareness of words—for example, rhyming and segmentation and the blending of separate sounds to form words—tends to be a more accurate predictor of beginning reading facility than either knowledge of word meaning or intelligence (Chall, 1967; Stanovich, 1991). Recent studies on adult illiterates and very poor readers (those below a fourth-grade level) find that they too have difficulty with phonics (Read & Ruyter, 1985; Strucker, 1995). It should be noted that knowledge of the meanings of words is perhaps a greater indicator of reading ability from about the third-grade level onward—that is, *after* the basic phonics skills have been acquired (Thorndike, 1913; Chall, 1983b).

Those concerned with phonological factors in reading view reading as developmental, with beginning reading different in its essentials from more mature reading. The whole-language proponents, in contrast, view both beginning and later reading as essentially the same process.

To sum up, the conception of beginning reading that gained acceptance in the late 1960s through the 1970s included phonological as well as cognitive and linguistic factors. By the 1980s through the 1990s, the whole-language movement brought back the original conception introduced in the 1920s, namely, that early reading facility is primarily dependent on age-appropriate language and sufficiently developed cognitive capabilities.

Research Evidence

Several syntheses of the research comparing the effectiveness, for learning to read, of a meaning (whole language) versus a code emphasis (phonics) were done by Chall in 1967 (covering the research from 1915 to 1965), in 1983 (covering the literature from 1967 to 1983), and in 1996 (covering the literature from 1983 to 1994). Other syntheses of the research have been done by Perfetti (1985), Feitelson (1988), Adams (1990), and most recently Snow, Burns, and Griffin (1998).

These syntheses found, in general, that classic approaches to beginning reading instruction (e.g., direct, systematic instruction in phonics—a code emphasis) were more effective than the various innovative approaches with which they were compared (e.g., a meaning emphasis, no phonics, incidental phonics, phonics only as needed, or a whole-language approach). The classic approaches were found to result in higher achievement in both word recognition and reading comprehension. They were more effective for different kinds of children and particularly for children at risk—those from low-income families, those of different cultural and ethnic backgrounds, bilingual children, and those with learning disabilities.

Did reading instructional practices change when the results of these studies became known? If so, did the changes in practice subsequently lead to positive changes in reading achievement? It is difficult to arrive at clear-cut answers to these questions, since it is hard to know specifically how reading instruction is practiced during given periods of time and in given places. Therefore, we must rely on indices that reflect practice. For *Learning to Read: The Great Debate* (1967), I made judgments about the use of given methods in schools during particular time periods by analyzing the reading textbooks and teacher's manuals that were in wide use at the time. I assumed that the methods in the most widely used teachers' manuals would serve as an index of practice.

Did the reading textbooks change? There is some evidence that they did. For the primary grades, the most widely used readers of the 1970s, as compared with those of the early 1960s, contained earlier and heavier instruction in phonics (Popp, 1975). The readers also contained more extensive vocabularies, grade for grade (an index of more challenging books). The reading textbooks of the 1980s, on the other hand, as compared with those of the 1970s, seemed to provide less instruction in phonics and heavier emphasis on reading comprehension and word meanings, even in the first grade. A recent analysis of current first-grade readers by Hoffman et al. (1993) found significantly more words than in readers published in 1986–1987, but the amount of instruction in phonics had declined further.

The Effects of Changed Practices on Students' Reading Proficiency

From 1971 to 1988, the National Assessment of Educational Progress made six separate national assessments of reading. Let us start with the NAEP scores for trends in reading achievement over the past twenty years and try to infer the possible influences of the new reading approaches on instructional practice and on student reading achievement.

From *The Reading Report Card, 1971–1988: Trends from the Nation's Report Card* (Mullis & Jenkins, 1990), we learn that from 1970 to 1980 there was steady improvement in reading comprehension for nine-year-olds. However, from 1980 to 1988 their scores did not improve and may even have declined: Nine-year-olds assessed in 1988 read significantly better than their counterparts assessed in 1971. However this progress was made during the 1970s (Mullis & Jenkins, 1990).

If we assume that practice followed the changes in emphasis of the basal readers for the primary grades, noted earlier, we have a hypothesis for the increases in the 1970s and the lack of improvement and possible declines of the 1980s. The NAEP scores of nine-year-olds (fourth graders) increased during the 1970s when the children were exposed as first and second graders to a stronger phonics component. And they ceased to improve and possibly declined in the 1980s when the phonics component in the early grades was less strong and the comprehension and word meaning components were greater. Thus, although the expectations of those holding the "new" viewpoints were that comprehension would increase when it was emphasized in the early grades, it would appear that the increased emphasis on comprehension in beginning reading textbooks and a decrease in phonics teaching may have led to decreases, not increases, in the reading comprehension of nine-year-olds. In contrast, the reading comprehension scores of the nine-year-olds during the 1970s increased when there was a stronger emphasis on learning letter–sound relationships and less focus on language and cognition in the early grades.

Are early advantages in reading maintained in later years? In the 1988 NAEP, increases found among seventeen-year-olds were attributed by the NAEP, at least in part, to the cohorts' early advantage, given their superior reading scores as nine-year-olds in the 1970s. Here again we have evidence that there was an increase in reading comprehension even among seventeen-year-olds when their beginning reading programs placed greater emphasis on phonological factors in the primary grades.

These findings from the NAEP generally confirm earlier studies—suggesting that one's reading capability is cumulative and developmental, and it needs different instructional emphases for different stages of reading development. Beginning reading may look the same as mature reading, but it is very different. Beginning reading has much to do with word recognition and phonics. It relies heavily on learning the relationship between spoken words and the letters and sounds that represent them. This is referred to as the alphabetical principal. As reading develops, it has more to do with language, experience, and reasoning (Chall, 1983b, 1996b; Chall, Jacobs, & Baldwin, 1990).

What does all this mean? First, it points to the importance of basing practice on sound theory and research that have been confirmed and reconfirmed over many years. The accumulated knowledge on reading proficiency suggests that (1) different aspects of reading be emphasized at different stages of reading development and (2) that success at the beginning is essential since it influences not only early reading achievement but also reading competency at subsequent levels of development. In short, a beginning reading program that does not give children knowledge and skill in recognizing and decoding words will ultimately produce poor results (see Adams, 1990; Chall, *Stages of Reading Development*, 1983b, 1996b; Stanovich, 1986).

In 1992, NAEP (see Mullis, Campbell, & Farstrup, 1993) collected data on classroom instructional practices in the fourth grade. The teachers described the amount of emphasis they placed on various approaches to teaching reading, including literature-based reading, integrating reading and writing, whole language, and phonics. The findings were that, at the fourth-grade level, fewer classes used a phonics emphasis as compared to using literature-based reading, integrated reading and writing, and whole language. The classes that emphasized phonics in the fourth grade also had the lowest achievers. Thus, the use of phonics in fourth grade with low achievers indicated that their teachers were aware that they were reading below expected levels and hence still needed instruction in phonics. For students making normal progress in reading, phonic instruction was no longer necessary. Thus, the NAEP findings can be used as additional support for the importance of learning phonics. The findings also confirm the wisdom of the long-established practice of emphasizing phonics in elementary school *remedial* programs.

The NAEP findings on reading proficiency for 1994 show little or no improvement among fourth graders and a decline among eleventh graders—suggesting that the whole-language and literature-based programs of the 1980s and 1990s, used when these students were in the primary grades, did not seem to raise their reading achievement.

The Role of Values and Ideologies

The foregoing findings, although based on recent research and surveys, were known at earlier times, based on earlier research and practice. My synthesis of the research from the early 1900s to 1996 (Chall, 1967, 1983a, 1996a) and that of Adams (1990) came to essentially the same conclusion, namely, that the more traditional methods of teaching reading in the primary grades (i.e., relying on phonics) result in better achievement. The early First Grade Studies of Bond and Dykstra (1967) found much the same to be true, as did the most recent synthesis of Snow, Burns, and Griffin (1998). Why, then, do we end up researching the same questions about beginning reading time and again? Why, one might reasonably ask, do we not accept the research findings and base our instruction on it?

For an answer to this question we must consider the other powerful forces (besides reason and common sense) that influence practice, namely, values, ideologies, philosophies, and appealing rhetoric. Since the early 1920s, at least, strong preferences have been expressed for reading methods that start with whole words or sentences, that is, an emphasis on *meaning*. In fact, some of these methods were adopted even during the great educational reforms of the early 1900s (as part of the early childhood education movement, progressive education, the child-centered movement, and the growing preference for informality). Although meaning-emphasis methods can be traced back even earlier, it was during the 1920s that they gained widespread favor and took on (even as they do today) all of the qualities and values of love, care, and concern for children. Proponents of these reforms claimed that reading for understanding right from the start was the best way to learn to read and to become a proficient reader as an adult. They abhorred rote learning. Concern with the phonological aspects of reading was seen then—as it is now, unfortunately—by whole-language proponents as pulling the reader away from understanding and toward rote learning. Therefore, it was to be avoided. The view in the 1920s was that concentrating on reading interesting stories (with little or no teaching of the sound-to-letter relationships of words) would result not only in better reading comprehension but also, ultimately, in a lifetime love of reading. Learning phonics was viewed as dull and dreary and as discouraging a wide range of reading and a lifetime love of it.

Although the research of the past eighty years has fairly conclusively refuted these claims against phonics, they nonetheless persist. If the claims are relinquished for a period of time, they still eventually return—as new discoveries, under new labels. Why are these mistaken views of phonics so persistent? I would suggest that it has much to do with most educators' preference for student-centered instruction. This conception promises that reading can be acquired without tears and that it is fun. Further, learning the relationships between letters and sounds does not require instruction, effort, and practice. The whole-language approach also promises more freedom for the child and the teacher, and certainly one aspect of student-centered methods is that they reduce comparisons between students since they are working on different "individualized" materials.

Thus, the one-stage theory of whole language seems to be more attractive to those teachers who prefer a more open, student-centered approach to education. Since whole-language proponents assume that reading instruction should be the same at the beginning as at the end, there is less need for knowing how it develops as students make progress. If teachers know the basic concepts about reading, some whole-language proponents would claim, they can teach beginners just as easily as advanced students.

The whole-language method, in particular, seems to say to teachers and parents that a good heart goes a long way—that is, the less formal the teaching, the better for the child. It's as though the method fears *structured* teaching more than *no* teaching. One of its main concerns is that the higher cognitive processes be used in reading, right from the start, and it avoids (by not confronting) the idea that there may be "basic skills" that do need to be learned early.

These are essentially student-centered views and they are being debated in other school subjects as well. In math, the current thrust is toward learning concepts instead of computation. In history, the concern is for teaching broad ideas, not facts. Although the NAEP findings indicate that our children have grave deficiencies in the most basic aspects of school subjects, the current focus is away from teaching these and toward teaching broader concepts and higher mental processes. As for reading, the preferred emphasis today remains on higher cognitive processes, right from the start, although some teachers are moving toward a greater emphasis on basic skills.

I propose that it is these views—views that focus on children's interests and choices and the development of their higher mental processes from the start (i.e., student-centered views)—that attracted teachers to the whole word and sentence methods of the 1920s and to whole language in the 1980s and early 1990s. It is a romantic view of learning. It is imbued with love and hope. But, sadly, it has proven to be less effective for reading achievement than a more traditional, teacher-centered view, particularly for those who are at risk while learning to read.

During the 1980s and 1990s, the prevailing ideology of reading has been one that views the child as self-motivated and joyous, a view similar to that of progressive educators of the 1920s. This view holds that a child learns to read as naturally as he learns to speak. He or she will learn if only we provide the books and the time to read them. Reading skills—especially those related to print and the sounds of words—are to be treated lightly, if at all, since they distract the learner from the naturalness of the reading process and the acquisition of meaning.

Very little is said about the children who have difficulty learning to read with this emphasis on language and cognition. When forced to confront the high incidence of failure from student-centered reading approaches, proponents answer that poor reading proficiency invariably stems from a limited literacy background or specific neurological or emotional difficulties.

The values and ideology I have briefly depicted can be found to underlie most reading programs from the 1920s until quite recently. From time to time there is a greater acceptance of the need for intensifying the teaching of basic skills when it is realized how many children are falling behind, as is now occurring with the sudden fall in reading scores in California, Texas, and other large states (Moats, 1997). Historically, however, these periods seem to be short-lived. Such a period existed during the 1970s, but by the 1980s the thrust was again toward the more romantic, charismatic, student-centered methods—that is, methods seen as natural and joyful.

The past several years have seen a pull toward stronger teacher-centered approaches in reading, with renewed emphasis on phonics and early preparation for learning of phonics through instruction in phonemic awareness. Thus, many of the most recent initiatives in reading instruction have inclined toward teacher-centered approaches. However, it should also be noted that whole-language methods are still favored by many teachers. Also, the student-centered emphasis of the 1980s and early 1990s seems to be retained in the descriptions of what should be taught, and when, that are contained in the national reading standards of the International Reading Association and similarly in many of the state standards.

AN OVERVIEW OF TRENDS
IN VARIOUS SCHOOL SUBJECTS

Overall, the reviews of mathematics, science, and social studies report similar broad trends. Generally, these subject areas moved from a more traditional, teacher-centered emphasis on knowledge and skills during the early 1900s to a more progressive, student-centered emphasis with concern for student interests and needs from the 1920s to the 1950s. During the late 1950s, following the launching of Sputnik, educators responsible for the teaching of math and science refocused more on the traditional, teacher-centered aspects of their subjects. Reading and social studies, on the other hand, continued their emphasis on motivation and interest.

From the 1970s through the 1990s, following widespread publicity over the low academic performance of U.S. students as compared to their Asian and European counterparts, greater emphasis began to be placed on raising academic standards for all students. More recently, all four subject areas have taken on a greater concern for higher order thinking and problem solving.

Within the past few years, there has been a growing interest in a greater teacher-centered emphasis for low achieving students. But this shift is not complete, since the state and national standards in the various subjects for fourth, eighth, and twelfth grades put a stronger emphasis on problem solving and creativity than on specific knowledge and skills.

TRENDS IN MATHEMATICS INSTRUCTION

In regard to student- versus teacher-centered approaches, the trends in twentieth-century mathematics instruction are similar to those in reading. During the early 1900s the emphasis was heavily teacher-centered. During the 1920s and 1930s greater interest was expressed in student-centered approaches, as evidenced through a greater concern with student readiness for mathematical learning, reducing the emphasis on computational skills, and increasing concern over young children's understanding of mathematical concepts. The 1920s, 1930s, and 1940s saw considerable curriculum development that was "decidedly in the direction of child understanding, in line with Dewey's general philosophy of child experience as the proper basis for learning" (Wilson, 1950, p. 48).

Another parallel with reading was that mathematics instruction was changing its *content* to more student-centered concepts. Thus, beginning around the 1920s and continuing until about the 1950s, greater interest was exhibited in a child's readiness for learning, problem solving, discovery, and exposing students to less difficult content.

The decline in mathematics proficiency during the late 1960s and early 1970s, which many attributed to the "new math," generated demands for "more traditional content goals and instructional methods" (Fey, 1982, p. 1167). This preference became even stronger during the 1980s, when U.S. children were found to achieve poorly in math as compared to European and Japanese students. On the international comparisons, eighth graders and twelfth graders in the United States showed less knowledge of math than students in most other countries in which the tests were given. "Even the best U.S. students (the top 1% and 5%) did poorly in comparison to the best students in other countries" (Fuson, 1992, p. 776).

Research on whether a teacher-centered or a student-centered approach leads to higher achievement in mathematics is quite sparse when compared to the research in reading. Fey notes that it has been difficult in the past to attribute cause-and-effect relationships to the teaching and learning of mathematics and subsequent achievement outcomes. However, some of the research is suggestive. For elementary schools some studies found that students in more "modern," student-centered programs did less well on computation than those in more traditional programs, but they did better on comprehension and problem solving (Fey, 1982).

Still other studies found an advantage of expository teaching (teacher-centered) for immediate recall, while discovery teaching (student-centered) was superior for retention and transfer. It was further found that the different methods worked best with different students, depending on their prior knowledge or ability: "weaker students seemed to benefit from expository teaching and stronger students from discovery" (Fey, 1982, p. 1177). Again, these findings were similar to those for reading instruction in that students lagging in achievement benefited from a teacher-directed emphasis.

Thus, it appears again that knowledge of basics is essential for more advanced progress.

In general, for the elementary grades, instruction that was task focused (teacher-centered), including "daily review, careful attention to development of meaning and understanding, closely monitored seatwork, and regular homework assignments," was found to be more effective than open student-centered teaching (Fey, 1982, p. 1178).

In spite of the positive findings for more teacher-centered mathematics education, there was a strong preference among some teachers for a student-centered focus with a particular preference for teaching mathematics as a high-level, problem-solving activity. The national standards for mathematics first published in 1989 had a strong student-centered, cognitive base (see Gardner, 1998, and Cheney, 1997).

Fuson noted that lower-achieving children and novices may require more structured experiences (teacher-centered), whereas higher achieving and more advanced students may learn better in a more self-directed (student-centered) environment (Fuson, 1992).

According to Gardner, the late 1990s brought a return to an interest in a more classic, teacher-centered approach in mathematics teaching, away from "fuzzy" math with its emphasis on solving problems "in the context of real world situations." Supported by complaints from parents that their children were unable to do the simplest mathematical calculations, as well as the support of distinguished scientists who opposed the student-centered methods, California turned away from the new math (Gardner, 1998).

Another late-1990s initiative for a stronger teacher-centered emphasis emanated from the National Council of Teachers of Mathematics, as elaborated in a November 1998 *Education Week*:

> The National Council of Teachers of Mathematics is proposing changes to its groundbreaking 1989 academic standards that would place a greater emphasis on teaching basic skills while reaffirming the group's belief that students need hands-on experience to help them understand mathematics facts. (Hoff, 1998, p. 1)

In the same issue of *Education Week*, Herbert J. Walberg proposed, on the basis of considerable research evidence, that academic achievement could be improved by using such well-known traditional practices as external incentives, homework, adherence to strict attendance rules, and grading individual, not group, accomplishments. These practices have long been associated with the traditional, teacher-centered approach, which Walberg contrasted with the less effective student-centered approach, in his view.

Summary of Instructional Trends in Mathematics

From the early 1900s to the present, the emphasis in mathematics education has moved from a traditional, teacher-centered pattern to a progressive, student-centered emphasis. There were brief "returns" to more teacher-centered approaches in the 1970s, following the disappointing results attributed to the "new math," and in the 1980s, when U.S. students were found to be achieving lower in math than most European and Japanese students. But these reversions to a stronger teacher-centered emphasis were relatively short-lived. By the 1990s mathematics seemed to be returning again to a greater student-centered emphasis—but one that stresses from the start the importance of problem solving and applications to real-life situations. This is seen in the changes to the math standards proposed in 1998 by the National Council of Teachers of Mathematics.

Overall, the evidence on the superiority of either a teacher-centered or a student-centered emphasis is limited as compared to that for reading. But the findings that exist and the observations made seem to be similar to those for reading, demonstrating an overall advantage for a teacher-centered emphasis, especially in instructing those making slower progress. Similarly, too, more able students tend to do well in programs that emphasize problem solving and creativity.

TRENDS IN SCIENCE INSTRUCTION

Science education came relatively late to U.S. schools, with one observer noting at mid-century: "until recently there has been but little provision for continuity in the study of science from elementary through secondary schools" (Powers, 1950, p. 1133). However, with the increased uses of science in industry and medicine, and the advent of both the space age and the computer age, interest in science education increased rapidly in the second half of the twentieth century.

The major concerns of science educators from 1900 to 1940 were what to teach, when, and what the textbooks should contain. Science educators of the early 1900s (as are those of today) were striving to meet two somewhat conflicting goals: (1) to adequately prepare elementary school children and then high school students for the rigors of college-level science; and (2) to make science education of interest and utility for students of all levels of ability (Powers, 1950).

The main goal during the early 1900s was just to get science taught. Concerns over whether science education should emphasize the use of modern, informal methods or classic, teacher-centered methods came much later.

Overall the early trends in science education were similar to those in math education and, as we will see later, in social studies. Preferences gravitated away from the learning of facts and information and toward the learning of principles and generalizations; away from the teaching of abstractions and toward the teaching of how science related to student needs and interests (i.e., social uses and applications).

These differences were grounded in the underlying evolving educational philosophies and preferences. When schools focused on a formal science curriculum, "the content of what is to be learned became the key focus for planning science instruction," but when socialization was seen as the main function of schooling, instruction focused on "science as it related to the whole child" (Butts, 1982, pp. 1665–1666).

In the late 1950s, following Sputnik's launching, science instruction changed its focus from developing "better participants in a democracy" to providing "scientists and engineers" (Butts, 1982, p. 1666). The science curriculum was then radically refashioned to reflect national priorities for scientific competency more so than students' social needs.

With regard to whether a teacher-centered or a student-centered emphasis is superior for student achievement in science, one study found that "directed study, with attention centered upon certain skills and techniques, resulted in achievement of a higher level than was attained through undirected study" (Powers, 1950, p. 1139). Another found that more traditional "lecture-demonstration" (teacher-centered) science programs resulted in greater achievement than the more active modern (student-centered) approaches. "Hands-on" teaching was found to be of secondary importance because it placed a "very heavy demand on the teacher" (Butts, 1982, p. 1667).

Although there was concern that science should be related to the daily life of the student, most secondary schools in the late 1970s did not offer such courses. In addition, most textbooks focused on knowledge used for careers in science.

In the 1990s the need for science education to accommodate the growing number of diverse ethnic groups became ever more evident. "These groups have not been major participants in science programs, and efforts to bring them fully into a science and mathematics curriculum has not been an important goal of elementary or of secondary schools" (Rowe, 1992, p. 1172). Another problem of the 1990s was the "comparatively poor performance of U.S. students at the fifth-grade level and all grade levels beyond the fifth on the Second International Science Study (SISS 1988) of the International Association for the Evaluation of Educational Achievement (IEA)" (Rowe, 1992, p. 1172). As a means of improving science achievement, Rowe suggests "increasing early exposure to the kinds of science experience and discussions that develop analytic and proportional reasoning" (Rowe, 1992, p. 1174).

As with reading and mathematics, science educators in the late 1990s are calling for a return to a greater emphasis on content—specifically, more challenging content (Olson, 1998).

Summary of Instructional Trends in Science

The trends in science instruction resemble somewhat those for reading and math, specifically, a heavy emphasis on content in the early 1900s and a shift, around the 1940s, to a greater concern for the scientific interests and needs of individual children (the student-centered emphasis). However, during the late 1950s, in the wake of Sputnik, there was an abrupt shift to greater concern for content (a teacher-centered emphasis) and for the stepped-up education of competent scientists—in response, no doubt, to Sputnik.

Beginning in the 1970s, there was growing concern that certain students were not studying science—whether women, ethnic minorities, or others—all of whom will need to know science as citizens, and many of whom will need to know it, hopefully, as scientists. This concern has continued and seems to be growing during the 1990s.

Overall, as with math and reading education, the student-centered pattern seems to have taken on greater importance in science from the 1920s onward. From time to time, however and especially from the late 1950s until the late 1990s—many science educators have called for a more teacher-centered pattern for educating scientists and engineers. This outcry for professional competency became particularly strong when U.S. students were found to lag significantly behind European and Asian students on international tests of scientific knowledge.

Few studies compared the achievement of students exposed to either a teacher-centered or a student-centered approach. The few that have been reported found results similar to those in reading, namely, that teacher-centered approaches were more conducive to superior academic achievement than student-centered approaches.

TRENDS IN SOCIAL STUDIES INSTRUCTION

The trends in teaching social studies from 1900 to the present mirror quite closely those observed for reading, mathematics, and science, namely, the gradual progression from a predominantly teacher-centered to a predominantly student-centered emphasis. However, in spite of this, little data exist on the relative effectiveness of teacher- versus student-centered emphases in social studies.

As early as the 1920s and 1930s, a greater emphasis was placed on child-oriented approaches to teaching social studies, with a greater concern for experiential learning, field trips, and participation in community activities. By the 1940s and 1950s, social studies textbooks put more emphasis on functional materials and less on detailed facts than the texts of the preceding generation (Carr, Wesley, & Murra, 1950).

Between 1920 and 1960, the teaching of social studies was "particularly susceptible to the ideology of progressive education on the elementary level" (Ponder & Davis, 1982, p. 1724), as was the teaching of reading, language arts, science, music, health, and art. And, in the 1970s, concern over declining test scores led to a greater emphasis on specific social studies skills, such as map and chart reading, and a deemphasis of the study of personal values.

Social studies has been viewed as having a traditional approach and a critical thinking approach. These two approaches can also be thought of as expository versus inquiry–discovery methods and are also reminiscent of the classic and progressive approaches—our teacher-centered and student-centered patterns.

Similar to a classic pattern,

> Expository instruction aims more toward information-acquisition tasks (recall, comprehension, or application) than does inquiry or discovery. . . . In contrast to exposition, discovery or inquiry instruction is more concerned with thought processes than with information acquisition. (Ponder & Davis, 1982, pp. 1727–1728)

Also of concern in the 1990s was "the adequacy of the dominant curriculum mode of elementary school social studies, one variously referred to as the *expanding environments, expanding horizons*, or *near to far* curriculum plan"—a model that "remained virtually unchanged as the dominant social studies curriculum plan for more than 50 years" (Crabtree, 1992, p. 1230). This model is based on the assumption that "young children's interests and developing capacities for social learning are centered in the here and now and only gradually, over successive years, expand to include the widening communities of which they are also members" (p. 1230). Much of the criticism against the use of the "expanding environment curriculum" came from studies that found that many children in the primary grades already knew what the primary curriculum and textbooks were attempting to teach them.

Why did the "expanding environments" model endure for so long in spite of growing discontent with it? Many factors were involved. Perhaps of foremost importance was the child-centered movement and progressive education in the 1930s, which reduced the historical content of social studies and increased the "social functions orientation" (Crabtree, 1992, p. 1231).

The expanding environments model finally lost its dominance

in the 1980s. The arguments for the abandonment of the model were advanced by Jerome Bruner, Bruno Bettelheim, Philip Phenix, and Diane Ravitch, among others. Many observers noted that "neither research in developmental psychology nor in children's learning supported the expanding environments model, which they found to be in violation of known principles of learning" (Crabtree, 1992, p. 1321). "In its stead, both Phenix and Bettelheim proposed the importance of history and literature in their power to enlarge children's experience, provoke their minds, awaken consciousness, and develop their appreciation of values and their vision of greatness" (p. 1321).

Other attempts to reform social studies education came from followers of Piaget (given their concern for cognition). Indeed, research has shown that strong knowledge of a field, as opposed to weak knowledge, leads to better integration and the ability to make inferences (Crabtree, 1992). It is important to note that, as the major objective of social studies moves from social problems to understanding, the role of knowledge takes on greater importance.

Similar to research in mathematics and reading, research in social studies education has found that cognitively challenging activities are positively related to children's interest and involvement.

Summary of Instructional Trends in Social Studies

Much as with our three other subject matters, social studies education during the past century moved from a teacher-centered emphasis on facts and knowledge in the early 1900s to a more student-centered focus. In the case of social studies, however, the latter phase began strongly in the 1920s, owing to the overarching influence of the philosophy of progressive education, with its emphasis on student needs and interests. This focus, which also included the model of the expanding curriculum—a curriculum that starts with the familiar, the home and the community, moving outward to the less familiar geographically and experientially—lasted for about fifty years. Beginning in the late 1970s, in response to the low achievement of students in social studies, the focus turned more to the academic and traditional, with a greater emphasis on teacher-centered approaches.

CHAPTER 5

◆

Research on the Overall Effects of Teacher- and Student-Centered Educational Programs

Is there valid evidence that one educational approach is better for academic achievement than the other—that the more open student-centered education is the better route to learning? Or do students do better when they are taught by means of a more traditional, teacher-centered approach? Given the intense debate over the past century about the two ways of educating students, one would expect to find vast amounts of research that tell us which is better. Yet, the extent of the research is modest and somewhat late in coming. But, as will be seen, the findings are quite consistent.

I present the evidence in two chapters. Chapter 5 reviews the findings of quantitative research that compares the results of a teacher-centered with a student-centered education. In such studies all conditions are kept similar. Only the educational approach is varied. Included are comparisons among private, parochial, and public schools as well as between Asian and U.S. schools.

Chapter 6 reviews the findings from several qualitative studies and descriptive reports of early experiments with student-centered education.

QUANTITATIVE COMPARISONS IN THE ELEMENTARY GRADES

One of the earliest and largest comparisons of teacher-centered and student-centered approaches in the early grades was conducted by Follow Through, a large-scale compensatory education program that extended Head Start through the third grade. It studied the effectiveness of three instructional models: a direct teaching model (teacher-centered), a cognitive model, and an affective teaching model (both student-centered). Each model was implemented in a variety of settings in schools with low-income children.

Stallings (1975) and ABT Associates (1977) found higher achievement in reading, math, and language for the direct instruction model as compared to the cognitive and affective models. Although the teacher-centered model produced higher results than the student-centered model, there was much skepticism and discontent with these findings. Much of the criticism related to statistical issues and the research design, with one critic suggesting that "Unique features of the local settings had more effect on test scores than did the models" (House, Glass, McLean, & Walker, 1978, p. 156). Others argued, on the basis of the same data, that the results supported highly structured educational approaches for teaching basic academic skills (Hayes & Wuerst, 1969).

Kennedy of the U.S. Office of Education (1978) concluded that the less effective education programs for disadvantaged children were those where the children were the planners and the teachers acted as facilitators of their learning. The programs showing a positive effect held the opposite philosophy, namely, that the teacher is the planner and controller of the children's learning. "The teacher centered models are oriented toward the basic skills, and these are the areas in which their positive effects occur" (Kennedy, 1978, p. 7).

In 1996 Adams and Engleman came to essentially the same conclusions in a summary of their numerous studies over a period of many years on Distar. entitled *Research on Direct Instruction: 25 Years Beyond Distar* (Distar—Direct Instructional System of Teaching Arithmetic and Reading—consists of a series of scripted, structured lessons conducted daily by teachers with small groups of children). They found that children who were taught with direct instruction did significantly better academically than those who were taught by any other means. In addition, they found benefits of direct instruction for social factors as well. And most of the benefits were found for poor children.

The authors present a variety of data on the effectiveness of direct instruction as compared to more open instruction—comparisons of simple means, of statistically significant outcomes, meta-analysis results, effect size by regular and special education students, and the like. Although some of these measures show stronger effects than others, all comparisons show that direct instruction (teacher-centered) models were superior for achievement than were open (student-centered) models.

It is important to note that in 1999 Distar was found to be among the three most highly validated school reform programs among twenty-four evaluated for effectiveness (Olson, 1999).

Of interest, too, is Adams's disappointment that direct instruction receives practically no attention in the regular education literature, although "direct instruction was the unanimous selection of our national panel of ten experts." When he mentioned it to the professors and students at the university where he was teaching, he was amazed at the hostility it generated. "I had heard similar negative comments for years and most of these comments were outrageously untrue" (Adams & Engleman, 1996, p. v).

Neville Bennett's (1976) comparison of open schools with more traditional schools found that formal teaching produced higher achievement. The methodology of the study was highly criticized by other researchers, however, and Bennett ended up agreeing that no conclusions could be drawn from his research.

GAGE'S SYNTHESES

In 1978 Gage published his first synthesis of quantitative studies done in the elementary grades and found that, in general, students in those schools that were more open (student-centered) had lower academic achievement than those in traditional (teacher-centered) schools. Further, the traditional instruction was especially beneficial for children of low-income families. For middle-class children, academic achievement was often the same for student-centered and teacher-centered programs. But overall, all children, including middle-class children, seemed to do better in traditional programs.

In a later synthesis, Gage and Berliner (1992) concluded that the effects of open education were not consistent and that there were only slight differences in academic achievement between teacher-centered (traditional) and student-centered classes. But they did find some small advantages for affective nonacademic outcomes in student-centered classes.

Perhaps more importantly, there were differences by social class. The middle-class children tended to achieve as well in the progressive as in the traditional schools. But the lower-class children did considerably better in the traditional schools (Gage, 1978).

Gage's 1978 synthesis also failed to find what many researchers had expected, namely, that children whose teachers asked more thought questions had greater understanding of the subject matter. Actually, he found precisely the reverse—that higher proportions of lower-order, or recall, questions led to higher scores on knowledge and understanding of the subject matter (see also Rosenshine, 1976, pp. 355–356).

Gage also cites Rothenberg (1989), who, like Cuban (1990), concluded that progressive education (student-centered) was not widely practiced. It was not practiced because it was very demanding of teachers and did not seem to improve achievement, on average. In addition, open education seemed to promise more than it could deliver. And it was often opposed in schools with many low-income and minority students, where parents saw it as neglecting basic skills, fostering chaos, and experimenting on their children (see Roland Barth, 1972).

Student-centered education, Gage noted, prepared teachers inadequately and was used without integrating its elements into a unified approach. It was inadequately monitored, thus allowing teachers and students to neglect important parts of the curriculum, especially basic skills (Gage & Berliner, 1992; in the next chapter I discuss a similar criticism of Gary student-centered schools that was made nearly a century earlier).

Gage was especially concerned about the possible negative effects of student-centered classrooms on the academic achievement of children from low-income families. As we saw in Chapter 4, studies of reading have consistently found higher reading achievement for low-income children in traditional, teacher-centered classrooms.

GOOD AND BROPHY

Good and Brophy's synthesis of quantitative studies in 1987 generally confirmed Gage's 1978 synthesis; they found that the best evidence overall indicated that open education was inferior to traditional education for student achievement. They also concluded, however, that open education may be somewhat superior in its effects on attitude and affective variables.

Good and Brophy also note that student-centered educational settings may be more effective for students who have the ability and motivation to work independently of direct teacher supervision most of the time. Student-centered education, however, presents difficulties for low achievers and others who need frequent teacher instruction and monitoring. This is true particularly for hyperactive students, who have difficulty sustaining concentration, as well as for students who lack interest and the self-discipline to sustain involvement in academic activities.

In summing up their research synthesis, Good and Brophy conclude that in general they were more impressed with the potential disadvantages of student-centered education than with its advantages.

> It seems clear that some degree of teacher structure is needed to promote both achievement gains and personal growth. The degree of structure needed will vary with the goals being pursued (subject matter achievement, for example, demands more structure than most goals) and with the ages and backgrounds of the students. (Good & Brophy, 1987, pp. 380–381)

ROSENSHINE'S STUDIES

Rosenshine's studies and syntheses of instruction in the elementary school also present important data on teacher-centered and student-centered approaches.

In a 1981 research synthesis Stevens and Rosenshine concluded that "Effective instruction is characterized by considerable teacher-led instruction directed at either the whole class or a small group of students" (p. 2). Although one-to-one instruction is normally effective and beneficial, it is *not so* in classes of twenty or more students since under those circumstances each child receives little one-to-one instruction—only three minutes per hour—and would be expected to work alone the remaining fifty-seven minutes. One-to-one instruction in large classes is less effective than desirable because "research results have consistently shown that students are more engaged when working in groups than they are when alone" (Stevens & Rosenshine, 1981, p. 2). Overall, students who worked in groups under adult supervision had higher achievement than those who worked alone. And students in classes where there was a strong emphasis on working alone were least engaged and achieved less. One advantage of grouping, according to Rosenshine, may be that, when working in groups, students receive more teacher demonstration and corrective feedback than when they are working alone.

Stevens and Rosenshine's explanation of why teacher-centered instruction leads to higher achievement is reminiscent of the explanation of its superiority noted in studies on the results of the Follow Through program (see page 80):

> In reading and math, students make more progress when the teacher, not the student, selects and directs the activities, and acts as a strong leader . . . approaches the subject matter in a direct, businesslike way, organizes learning around questions posed by the teacher, and occupies the center of attention. (1981, p. 2)

It is important to note that the "directive" teacher is not usually the ideal teacher in a student-centered classroom. The ideal teacher for student-centered approaches is someone who "facilitates" and "guides."

A recent study of Reading Recovery—a one-on-one tutoring program for first grade children found that the stronger and more directive the Reading Recovery teacher, the higher the student's reading gains (Chall, 1996a).

With regard to individualization of instruction, Stevenson and Rosenshine found that students working alone, on tasks of their own choosing, do not do as well as when they work in groups.

The kinds of questions asked by the teacher and the frequency of the questions and correct responses were important for achievement, particularly for low-income students. The benefits of asking higher-level questions were not supported, however. Instead, similar to Gage (1978), they found that, "asking different numbers of higher level questions had no measurable effect on essay performance or performance on tests containing higher level questions" (Stevens & Rosenshine, 1981, p. 5).

In a more recent synthesis of the research on teaching, Rosenshine notes that the results are applicable to any explicit "well-structured" body of knowledge when the objective is to teach skills based on a body of knowledge. They are less applicable for teaching content that is less well structured or where skills do not follow explicit steps or concepts, for example, writing term papers, reading comprehension, analysis of literature, or discussion of social issues or concepts.

Research on the effectiveness of teacher-centered or student-centered approaches to problem solving has been less extensive than the research on skills and knowledge. But it does show that well-organized background knowledge and fluency in skills and procedures are needed for effective problem solving. The learning of higher-level cognitive skills does not entail dropping the learning of facts and skills. Indeed, according to the Rosenshine and Meyers synthesis, facts and skills are *both necessary* for the meaningful development of higher-level cognitive skills.

Rosenshine's most recent synthesis, from 1980 to 1994, covers research on higher-order cognitive strategies (Rosenshine & Meister, 1994). To teach cognitive strategies effectively, the research suggests providing students with a variety of support structures, or "*scaffolds.*" Provided by the teacher or another student, these help to bridge the gap between current abilities and the intended goal. They provide adjustable and temporary support that can be removed when no longer needed.

It is often assumed that higher-level cognitive strategies do not require systematic teaching and practice, since they cannot be taught as explicitly as more structured tasks. Yet, the relevant research evidence finds that a great deal of student practice *is* needed. At the beginning, most of the task is completed by the teacher through modeling and thinking aloud (scaffolding). As students progress, they take on more and more responsibility for the task, and gradually the teacher's support is withdrawn (Rosenshine & Meister, 1994).

The teaching of higher-order cognitive strategies, according to Rosenshine and Meister, is similar in many ways to direct instruction or explicit teaching. Indeed, they say, there is no conflict with the work on direct instruction. The results of the research suggest a continuum rather than a dichotomy—from well-structured, explicit skills to less structured tasks. At all points along the continuum some instructional elements, such as presenting information in small steps and providing guided practice, are important. As the students move from well-structured to less structured cognitive strategies, they need more scaffolds, such as models, prompts, or hints (Rosenshine & Meister, 1994).

COMPARISONS WITH ASIAN SCHOOLS

Achievement differences between U.S. and Asian students are also instructive for understanding the effects of the teacher-centered and student-centered educational approaches on academic achievement. There is a general consensus that Asian education is more traditional than ours. Asian students have a more demanding curriculum, grade for grade, and a longer school year than we do.

There is also a widespread view that Asian schools rely mainly on rote learning while ours rely more on thinking and creativity, although there is considerable difference of opinion on this. There is greater agreement that our schools are less demanding and rely more on student's interests and on encouraging individual differences. Asian parents also demand more home study time and send students to extra "cram" schools on weekends. Thus, in terms of our two educational approaches, teacher-centered and student-centered, Asian schools appear to fit better the model of traditional, teacher-centered education while our schools have a better fit with the more progressive, student-centered education.

The study *The Learning Gap: Why Our Schools Are Failing and What We Can Learn from Japanese and Chinese Education*, by Harold Stevenson and James Stigler (1992), treats these differences in great detail and with sensitivity. During the 1980s Stevenson and his associates gave mathematics and reading tests to first graders and fifth graders in the United States, Japan, and China. In addition, they made similar extensive observations of classrooms and interviewed parents in all three countries.

Their major finding was that, on tests of mathematics achievement for both the first and fifth grades, the scores of American children were far lower than those of their Japanese and Chinese peers. This was not a new finding; earlier studies had reported similar results:

> Data from the Second International Mathematics Study show that the performance of the top 5 percent of U.S. students is matched by the top 50 percent of students in Japan. Our very best students—the top 1 percent—scored lowest of the top 1 percent in all participating countries. (summary of National Research Council's report "Everybody Counts," cited in Stevenson & Stigler, 1992, p. 31)

Another study that assessed the mathematical competence of thirteen-year-olds in Korea, Spain, the United Kingdom, Canada, Ireland, and the United States found that students from the United States had the lowest average scores of all the children (Stevenson & Stigler, 1992, p. 31).

These studies also found that the low mathematics scores of U.S. students, which begin in the early elementary grades, become even more deficient in the higher grades.

Achievement in reading was somewhat different. The average reading achievement of Asian and U.S. children in the fifth grade was not as discrepant. However, the American children were overrepresented in both the better reader and poorer reader categories: "the number of American children among the worst readers greatly exceeded the number we would expect, if reading skills in the three cities were equivalent" (Stevenson & Stigler, 1992, p. 46). "Thirty-one percent of the American fifth graders, 12 percent of the Chinese, and 21 percent of the Japanese were judged to be reading at the third-grade level (two years behind the expected)" (p. 48; see also Venezky, 1997).

Of even greater interest are the differences in American and Asian educational values and practices. Many of these have become widely known and frequently cited. Perhaps the most dramatic is that Asian parents and teachers tend to view school achievement as an outcome of effort and hard work, while American parents put a greater emphasis on ability. Asian children tend to see school as central to their lives; U.S. students do not. Asian parents support their children's efforts by organizing the home environment to make it conducive to studying; parents in the United States do not. Asian teachers assign large amounts of homework, as early as the first grade, and Asian children spend considerable portions of their time getting it done. Mothers' estimates of time spent on homework by Japanese first graders were three times as high, and Chinese mothers' estimates seven times as high as for children in the United States (Stevenson & Stigler, 1992, pp. 54–55). Various surveys have found that U.S. students, especially those in the early grades, do little homework.

Many of the practices of Japanese schools cited by Stevenson and Stigler are reminiscent of practices that were popular in U.S. schools prior to the 1920s, when traditional, teacher-centered education was predominant—emphasis on hard work, correcting of errors, and homework.

There were also great differences in the time spent on various school activities in U.S. and Asian homes. Asian students spend more time at home at the desks that are set aside for school work, and they read more. Japanese children read for pleasure about 5.7 hours per week, Chinese children read 4.3 hours per week, and children in Minneapolis read 3.8 hours per week (Stevenson & Stigler, 1992, p. 59). The differences appear to widen in the later elementary grades. Asian children also read more adult newspapers, some of which include special pages written for children.

Most U.S. newspapers do not publish such special pages, but more are beginning to do so.

Additionally, there were differences in how order was maintained in classrooms. Asian teachers who have larger classes, with no tracking or separation by ability, maintain greater order and structure. They do so by teaching children techniques and skills to work effectively in a group and in large classes. Also, children stay with the teacher for two years. Most of the time the children work together with a teacher as leader, which "enhances students' feelings of group membership and reduces their sense of isolation." Children in the United States, on the other hand, spend considerable time working by themselves at their own pace. "This practice may have benefits, but working at one's own pace means working alone, and the slower one's pace, the more time spent alone" (Stevenson & Stigler, 1992, p. 65).

Stevenson and Stigler found that there was a sense of loneliness among the children in the United States because of the emphasis on individual work at an individual pace. The Asian children seem to be happier working as a class. Children in the United States are less likely to say they like school. For example, between 75 and 86 percent of the children in Japan, compared to 52 to 65 percent of U.S. children, indicated that they liked school.

It is ironic that the ideal in the United States of individualizing instruction, originally thought to bring greater desire for learning and higher achievement, is seen by Stevenson and Stigler as contributing to U.S. students' lack of enthusiasm for school and their lower academic achievement. The U.S. view on whole-class instruction since student-centered education became so popular is that the former results in regimentation, conformity, and lower achievement—hence, it is not to be used generally. Small groups and individualized instruction are to be used instead. And yet, visitors to Chinese and Japanese elementary schools are struck by the children's apparent pleasure and involvement in their schoolwork when they work as a class and in large groups (Stevenson & Stigler, 1992, p. 70).

The U.S. and Asian schools also differ considerably with regard to explicit teaching of routines and methods. In later grades, Asian children are taught to answer questions and take notes. Asian teachers explicitly teach the components of skills needed for the smooth operation of classroom routines (Stevenson & Stigler, 1992, p. 91).

U.S. teachers seldom directly teach classroom routines. Indeed, it has been the ideal in student-centered education that children discover, on their own, knowledge, skills, and also proper behavior. The fear of U.S. teachers is that they may direct too much, or teach too much, and thereby deny students their originality and freedom.

The same seems to be true of the way we view teachers and teaching. We often act as if good teachers are born, not made. Good teaching is viewed as "having a knack with children" and being able to keep them attentive and enthusiastic about learning. Many colleges of education view teaching as "an art that cannot be taught" (Stevenson & Stigler, 1992, p. 157).

In Asia, according to Stevenson and Stigler, the ideal teacher is a skilled performer. She tries to perfect each lesson using the teaching techniques she learned, interpreting them in a manner she thinks will interest and motivate her pupils.

U.S. teachers are more concerned with sensitivity and patience than Chinese teachers are. These attributes fit the emphasis in the United States on individual differences and self-esteem.

Chinese teachers, on the other hand, put greater emphasis on factors directly relevant to teaching subject matter, such as being able to explain things clearly and to be enthusiastic.

> In America, teachers are judged to be successful when they are innovative, inventive, and original. Skilled presentation of a standard lesson is not sufficient and may even be disparaged as indicating a lack of innovative talent. It is as if American teachers were expected to write their own play or create their own concerto day after day and then perform it with expertise and finesse. These two models, the skilled performer and the innovator, have very different value in the East and West. (Stevenson & Stigler, 1992, pp. 166–167)

Considerable differences were observed with regard to discipline. U.S. children talk to each other and wander around the classroom more than Asian children. And they fidget more and are more inattentive; thus, monitoring discipline is a difficult problem in America. It is easier for Japanese and Chinese teachers, because they rely on the children to monitor discipline. The following observation illustrates this dynamic in a Japanese first-grade classroom.

> The teacher tried to begin the daily mathematics lesson. The children were noisy and continued their loud conversations. The teacher paused, looked at the class, and then called on the child who was the day's classroom leader: "The children are too noisy. Until they are quiet, I cannot teach," she said matter-of-factly. The young leader went into action. She stood, faced the class, and announced, "Please stand up. We are so noisy, teacher can't teach." The children quickly became quiet. The leader turned to the teacher and reported: "We are quiet now." The children bowed to their teacher and sat down, attentive as the teacher announced, "We will begin." (Stevenson & Stigler, 1992, p. 171)

Walberg's Meta-Analysis: Elementary and High Schools

Herbert Walberg (1990) analyzed some 800 studies on the effects of teacher and methods factors on the educational achievement of elementary and high school students. He labeled most of the instructional methods or factors as either traditional (teacher-centered) or innovative (student-centered). Walberg found that some teaching techniques had enormous positive effects on achievement while others had only small advantages. Some, in fact, seemed to impede learning.

The methods that had the greatest positive effects on achievement were certain psychological elements of teaching based on the works of E. L. Thorndike and B. F. Skinner—cues, engagement, corrective feedback, and reinforcement. The effects were huge—from 0.88 to 1.25 standard deviations. While some of these psychological elements are found in both teacher-centered and student-centered classrooms, my guess is that they are more common in traditional, teacher-centered classes. Cues and engagement seem to require the teacher's direction. Hence, the methods that had the greatest effects fit better with the teacher-centered than with the student-centered education. Corrective feedback also seems to have a better fit with teacher-centered methods rather than with student-centered methods. The quick correction of errors and remedying of difficulties is usually more characteristic of teacher-centered than student-centered classes. Immediate and direct reinforcement, while used in both educational approaches, is probably used more widely in teacher-centered classes.

Other characteristics with positive effects on achievement that were associated more with teacher-centered than with student-centered classrooms were: the absence of irrelevant behavior, bridging from previous knowledge and from previous material, adjunct questions, frequent testing or quizzes, questioning in science, homework with teacher comments, homework with grades, remedial feedback in science, explicit and direct teaching (Walberg, 1990).

Some evidence was found, also, for the positive effects of the newer, student-centered methods: the science programs first instituted in the 1960s in response to Sputnik (new science curricula of the National Science Foundation) had many positive effects on creativity, problem solving, scientific understanding, spatial relations, subject attitude, and science attitude (Walberg, 1990).

Overall, the findings from Walberg's meta-analysis tend to confirm the results of the quantitative studies reported earlier. On the whole, teacher-centered classroom characteristics produced higher academic achievement than those favored by student-centered classrooms. Some student-centered characteristics, however, also produced advantages for creativity, problem solving, and attitudes toward science.

QUANTITATIVE COMPARISONS
OF THE HIGH SCHOOL GRADES

The research evidence presented in this section is based on comparisons of high school students in different kinds of schools in the United States—public versus private and parochial. I have included these studies because in a real sense they are natural experiments of the two educational patterns—the teacher-centered and student-centered.

Since the early 1920s private and parochial schools in the United States have tended to favor a teacher-centered approach, whereas the public schools have been more student-centered in their preferences and practices (Powell, 1996).

Probably the most celebrated quantitative study of high school students was the Eight-Year Study that compared students in experimental, progressive high schools (student-centered) with those in traditional (teacher-centered) schools. The study was started in 1930 and ran for roughly eight years, following the same students through high school and into college.

The Eight-Year Study was much more than a comparison of the two educational patterns. It was also very much concerned with the efforts of teachers and administrators to define the goals of progressive education and to determine how these were implemented in the classroom. This process is depicted with great enthusiasm in the published report of the findings (Ohio State University, 1940).

After much study by the Ohio State faculty, a number of principles became clear to them concerning an organized program of evaluation. The essential aspect was to make progress rather than status the basic criterion of evaluation and to specify that "interpretation of what the school experiences are doing and have done to the child becomes much more important than measuring what the child has done with subject matter" (Ohio State University, 1940, p. 35).

Scholarship, attendance, and deportment were not viewed as isolated items for measurement to be reported to parents. Instead, evaluation was to be "placed upon aspects of child development, of progress towards maturity in character, citizenship, personality, and problem solving" (Ohio State University, 1940, p. 35).

At the time, the findings of the Eight-Year Study were judged not to be as strong nor as clear-cut as was hoped for. No "significant" differences were reported. The report used such terms as "slightly more," "more often," and "a high degree of."

However, Cremin analyzed the findings twenty years later (Cremin, 1961) and reported that, when the graduates of the 30 progressive high schools in the study were in college, they earned a slightly higher total grade average than had those in the traditional schools and earned slightly more academic honors in each of the four years of college.

A less sanguine view of the Eight-Year Study findings is found in Angela Fraley's *Schooling and Innovation* (1981), written some four decades after the completion of the study. Noting the lack of certainty in its conclusions, Fraley wrote that after eight years the study's authors could state only that the students from experimental schools performed as well academically in college as their matches from conventional schools (Fraley, 1981, p. 125).

Fraley also made several critical comments on the study's research methods—that there was little attempt to control for the range of innovations among the experimental schools. Some deviated from standard practices quite a bit while others did less so. Actual innovative practices defied statistical comparison, not only among schools but also among classrooms within the same schools (Fraley, 1981, p. 126).

Coleman and Hoffer (1987) compared the achievement of high school students of similar abilities and backgrounds who attended private and parochial, versus public schools. The measures used to compare student achievement were gains over a two year period (from the sophomore to the senior year) on standardized achievement tests of reading, vocabulary, mathematics, science, civics, and writing. They found the achievement gains to be generally higher in the parochial and private schools than in the public schools. Catholic (parochial) and other private school students, at almost all levels of achievement, outperformed public school students when they were seniors. The greatest difference between parochial and public school students was in mathematics, whereas the greatest difference between other types of private versus public schools was in reading comprehension (p. 68). The extent of the difference in achievement was considerable—an achievement gain of about three grade equivalents in two years' time in the Catholic schools, compared to two grade equivalent gains in two years for the public school students (p. 92).

The reactions of the educational community to the Coleman and Hoffer study findings were far from favorable. Many criticized it, claiming that Catholic and other private schools had an advantage, since they could reject problematic students. Public schools had to admit and retain all who applied. Coleman replied that the higher achievement of the nonpublic school students was related to what was emphasized and valued in these schools—more structure, discipline, and homework—all of which had a high correlation with achievement in public as well as in private schools. The public schools could improve the achievement of their students, he claimed, by attending to these conditions. It was not a matter of private versus public schools but of what was done in the schools. It is structure, discipline, and homework that are important for student achievement, not whether the school is private or public.

Bryk, Lee, and Holland (1993) compared the achievement of Catholic high school students with comparable students in public schools. Throughout their report they emphasize the educational conditions, requirements, and curricula that distinguished the Catholic from the public schools they studied. Their goal was to find which of the schools were stronger or weaker in achievement and what the possible causes of these differences were. The comparisons were made only for mathematics because it is most strongly influenced by schooling and least by home factors.

Their findings were that, by the senior year high school students in Catholic schools from lower-middle-class homes were achieving 4.5 years ahead of their counterparts in the public schools. Upper-middle-class Catholic school students were 2.4 years ahead of comparable public school students (Bryk et al., 1993). Thus, while Catholic school students were generally several years ahead of public schools in math, the advantage was even greater for the less advantaged students. (See Powell, 1996, for similar findings in studies comparing public with private schools.)

Among the conditions in the Catholic schools that Bryk found to be associated with higher achievement were a predominance of required courses and a limited number and variety of electives. Catholic schools challenged the students more: the content of their courses was more advanced and, they studied subjects in greater depth than in the public schools.

With regard to the overall style of education of the Catholic schools, Bryk noted that, while they have made some accommodations to the new, progressive, open education, "they never moved so far or so firmly in that direction as did the public schools" (1993, p. 32). He noted that "the character of instruction in Catholic high schools appears quite traditional in format, setting, use of materials, and pedagogy" (p. 99).

Arthur Powell's recent study of private schools in the United States focuses on "the most significant features of the independent school tradition" in order to explore how "they might shed constructive light on important issues confronting all American schools," public and private (1996, p. 251). Powell states in his prologue that he has no interest in arguing the case for or against private schools. What interests him are the "lessons" that can be learned from privileged private schools that could be of benefit to all schools.

One of the lessons that Powell notes as being of great importance to all schools is the success of private schools with average students. While the most able students do achieve very well in private schools, it is the average student who achieves very much better than comparable students in public schools. According to Powell, privileged private schools have had extensive experience with typical, average or below-average college bound students.

> Affluent families for a century have wanted their children (especially their male children) to attend college regardless of capacity or interest. Many schools proudly regard the services they give to average students as their best, most distinctive, and most satisfying work. (1996, p. 166)

About 40 percent of students in private schools are of average ability, and with most seeking entrance to "good" colleges, the private schools adopted two contrasting approaches to maintaining academic standards. "One approach extends the old tradition of pressing all students regardless of aptitude, toward a relatively common academic standard and school experience" (Powell, 1996, p. 170). The second, newer, approach "regards standards as being, at least in part, unique to each individual . . . and schools should concentrate on developing the potentials of each one instead of insisting that everyone merely 'pass' at some arbitrary level" (p. 170). The independent schools began, belatedly, to accept the "individual's potential" as standard, but they never gave up on the older, more traditional, standards, as did most public schools. The strong academic push on all students comes also from a focused curriculum that most students experience together. All study algebra and several years of serious math—"all of them, even those to whom math does not come easily" (p. 173).

The independent school curriculum is also more limited than that of the public schools. Independent schools offer fewer courses, and the courses, even for the average students, are traditional and rigorous. "Average or below average students in prep schools are more likely to experience a challenging high school curriculum than are average but privileged college-bound students in public schools" (Powell, 1996, p. 177). Powell views the "limited curriculum" as an advantage, for it gives students a shared intellectual experience that they can discuss with one another, not possible when the curriculum is more individualized (p. 173).

Parents assume that students will perform differently in their studies because they are different. "But they assume they should 'all be performing the same' when it comes to working hard. 'The standard to which all kids should be held accountable is work effort'" (Powell, 1996, p. 178).

Private school students generally do more homework than public school students. According to Powell, "average prep school sophomores do more homework than any other group of American sophomores. This is surely because curriculum expectations for them have not been lowered, dumbed down, or made voluntary" (1996, p. 178).

There was some lowering of academic standards during the 1960s when private school students were more rebellious toward school authority. There was a greater interest in popular culture and a move toward a more relaxed and flexible atmosphere. Powell noted many changes, including: a reduction in pressure to do well, reductions in academic requirements (including lessened emphasis on skills and reading), a greater interest in pass–fail grading, an increase in curriculum electives, more minicourses and independent study, and more discussion and fewer lectures (p. 181).

But, Powell notes that this trend was reversed when the national SAT score decline was announced near the end of the 1960s. "Gradually it again became acceptable to talk favorably of high academic standards" (p. 182).

Powell attributes the high achievement of students in private schools to its classic curriculum, which all students, not only the most able, are required to study. In addition, choices are also available to meet individual student strengths and interests. All of this is supported by heavy homework assignments (heavier than for students of comparable ability who attend public schools) and smaller classes, which means more attention from teachers.

Overall, Powell paints a picture of private school students who work hard and long. For most students, classes are followed each day by sports or other extracurricular activities. With several hours of homework each night, there is hardly time to watch TV. Indeed, as teachers are discovering the great amount of "free time" of students in public schools has prompted some parents, especially when both work, to schedule after-school activities—such as reading a book, writing an essay, or playing an educational game—as a defense against their children's just "hanging out." Several of these "activities" are available commercially. Thus, it appears as though many parents are providing the rigor that the public schools have left behind.

SUMMARY OF FINDINGS FROM THE QUANTITATIVE STUDIES

The research comparing the effects on academic achievement of teacher-centered and student-centered educational practices has generally found the teacher-centered to be more effective. A few research studies that compared the effects on nonacademic learning were favorable toward the student-centered programs, but those advantages were less pronounced than the discrepancy in academic achievement.

Most of the studies that compared the effects of the two educational approaches on both middle and lower SES children found that the teacher-centered approaches were particularly beneficial for children of average or low socioeconomic status (Adams & Engleman, 1996). For middle-class children, the differences by educational approach were not as large or were nonexistent. Some studies noted that the student-centered learning may in fact be harmful for low SES students who are unable to take the responsibility necessary for effective learning under such conditions. These studies suggested that perhaps some things are learned and retained better when children are instructed directly (Gage, 1992, p. 487; see also Barth, 1972; Delpit, 1986).

Rosenshine's research confirms that the advantages of individualized learning—a different pace for different children, and choice of what to learn and how to learn it—characteristics of student-centered education, have not been borne out, especially for poor children. Learning in groups, and by the class, with teacher instruction and direction leads to higher achievement.

The methods with the highest positive effects on learning are those for which the teacher assumes direction, for example, letting students know what is to be learned and explaining how to learn it, concentrating on tasks, correcting errors, and rewarding of activities—characteristics found in traditional, teacher-centered education.

Thus it would appear that the hoped for academic improvement from student-centered education has not been fulfilled. While some student-centered approaches may have produced small gains in nonacademic characteristics, and in higher cognitive learnings as in high school science, they have usually resulted in lower academic achievement, particularly in the basic curriculum areas. Quite consistently, when results were analyzed by socioeconomic status, it was the more traditional education that produced the better academic achievement among children from low-income families.

Were there any consistent differences for age and grade? Were the results similar, for example, in both the high school and elementary grades? Because most of the studies were conducted on elementary, and fewer on high school, students, it is hard to draw any firm conclusions with regard to differences in effects by school level. But one can speculate that the effects are probably greater for the lower than the higher grades, one reason being that different learnings are stressed in the elementary grades than in high school. The elementary grades focus more on the acquisition of fundamental knowledge and skills, while high schools are more oriented toward reasoning and problem solving. This distinction fits Whitehead's characterization of learning by stages, starting with a romantic stage, moving to a stage of precision and knowledge, then to a stage of generalization and abstraction (see Hendley, 1986). It also fits Bloom's stages of exceptional achievement in sports, science, and the arts (see Bloom, 1985; Bloom & Sossriak, 1981), and my own stages of reading development, from learning to read to reading to learn.

It also fits the research evidence on the lower achievement at both elementary and high school levels among low socioeconomic status students and those who have difficulty learning. In a sense these students are functioning at a lower level of proficiency than others their age and seem to need the direction and structure of a teacher-centered approach. It may well be that the essential distinction in benefiting more from a traditional, teacher-centered approach is its greater provision of knowledge and skills needed at earlier stages of learning.

CHAPTER 6

—

Descriptive Studies of Early Educational Experiments

This chapter describes three educational experiments conducted in the late 1890s and early 1900s: at the Dewey Laboratory School in Chicago, Bertrand Russell's Beacon Hill School in Sussex, England, and the Gary schools of Gary, Indiana. I use these descriptive reports to determine how close their observations were to the findings from the quantitative, controlled studies reported in Chapter 5. I include them also because of the rich insights they provide into the strengths and weaknesses of the student-centered educational approaches the schools represented.

Both the Dewey and Russell schools were planned and directed by philosophers and were run by husband-and-wife teams, and in both schools the founders' children were enrolled as students. Their missions, although not entirely the same, had many important features in common. Both were strong advocates of freedom for the children, the teachers, and the curriculum, and both came into existence in opposition to traditional education.

DEWEY'S LABORATORY SCHOOL

The Laboratory School at the University of Chicago, which ran from 1896 to 1904, was headed by John Dewey. Planned as a means for relating theory to practice, it held long discussions with teachers on whether practice was in line with the theory of the school. Unfortunately, it did not keep sufficiently detailed records from which assessments of its effectiveness could be objectively drawn. However, several published reports, as well as informal comments about the school by parents and teachers—as well as Dewey's comments—give some rich descriptions of the school's effectiveness.

It is important to note that the school was small. It started with sixteen students and two teachers and reached its maximum size in 1902 with a student enrollment of 140 and a faculty of twenty-one.

Dewey compared the Laboratory School to that of laboratories in biology, physics, or chemistry, and, like such laboratories, it had two main purposes:(1) to exhibit, test, verify, and criticize theoretical statements and principles; and (2) to add to the sum of facts and principles.

The students in the school came mainly from professional families. Most were children of the faculty of the University of Chicago—from middle- or upper-class backgrounds. And the vast majority of parents were strong supporters of the school.

"Dewey . . . frequently argued against resorting to heavy-handed discipline, memorization, or even sugar-coating the material in order to arouse the child's interest" (Hendley, 1986, p. 23). Genuine interest, he held, meant that the child was wholeheartedly involved in what he or she was doing. The subject matter to be learned could not be a substitute for the child's experience. Nor could it be simply imposed upon him or her. Hendley asserts that Dewey did not advocate a strictly child-centered approach to education, as was often assumed, nor did he downplay the curriculum to be studied, since it represented our intellectual and cultural heritage. What he objected to was forgetting that subject matter stems from human experience (Hendley, 1986).

Thus, Dewey wanted his school to be neither child-centered nor curriculum-centered, but he insisted that it was the process of learning, rather than its products, that was most important. He also held that the scientific attitude of mind was particularly worthy of promotion. He also sought to make the school a community in which teacher and student are mutually engaged in inquiry, in directly experiencing rather than passively memorizing second-hand experience (Hendley, 1986).

The children in the school fell within the ages of four to fifteen. They were divided into eleven groups according to age, and from the very start the emphasis was on social aspects of learning. But one could not say from the following activities that it was not also concerned with content.

The six-year-olds spent the first fifteen minutes of the day in group conversation. They took excursions, played floor games, built a farm house and barn out of blocks. They planted cotton seeds in pots and ginned and baled the cotton. The seven-year-olds began to study primitive life. They studied the use of textiles and the discovery of metals.

The eight-year-olds worked on trading and maritime activities of the Phoenicians. This made them aware of the need for a system of weights and measurements and for a more accurate method of keeping written records. They studied the life and voyages of Christopher Columbus and began to read *Robinson Crusoe*. This was in accord with Dewey's desire to avoid teaching reading and writing too soon (Hendley, 1986, p. 28). Dewey was concerned about using the child's analytic and abstract "powers" prematurely. He advocated for starting with activities that would engage the child's creative impulses "and direct them in such ways as to discipline them into the habits of thought and action required for effective participation in community life" (p. 28). Dewey saw the importance of studying language to provide discipline, organization, and the effective means of communication, but he was adamant that it not be taught until the child was able to recognize his or her own need for it.

The nine-year-olds had a longer school day in order to have more time to practice reading and writing. They also studied local history and geography. "The children were said to be anxious to attain greater facility in writing and number work in order to carry on their projects to a desired conclusion" (Hendley, 1986, p. 29).

The ten-year-olds studied colonial history and built a colonial room. The eleven-year-olds studied the European backgrounds of the colonists. The twelve-year-olds were concerned with the nature of occupations and saw the need for certain skills to achieve desired results.

The thirteen-year-olds reviewed U.S. history. Each child was urged to select books that were listed, to seek his or her own sources, and to get the help of parents and friends in writing about a topic. The fourteen- and fifteen-year-olds were given special tutoring and review courses to prepare them for college board examinations.

Throughout the school year the teachers held weekly meetings to review, discuss, and improve the past week's work. They also met daily during lunch and after school. They worked so hard to meet the demands of the program that several left the school because of exhaustion.

The teachers were better trained and more committed than would normally be found in schools at that time, and the teacher–pupil ratio was very low, with about seven students per teacher. Most teachers were strong supporters of the school and what it was trying to achieve. The majority of parents were also strong supporters of the school—morally and financially. One parent was so enthusiastic he became a teacher of history at the school. Generally, there was much enthusiasm about what the school was doing and about its future.

But, not all of the parents were pleased with it. "One father made this caustic comment about his son's experience there: 'One year at the University Preparatory Laboratory . . . nearly ruined him. We have to teach him how to study. He learned how to observe last year' " (p. 20).

Another concern was with the way the school prepared the older students for college entry. At ages fourteen and fifteen, the students were given special tutoring and review courses to prepare for their college board examinations. One visitor to the school said he was disturbed when he saw three or four students being drilled for college examinations "in the old way." Initially, he was disappointed that the regular work of the Laboratory School failed to prepare students for such tests. But he changed his mind: "As I considered the matter on my way home, I satisfied myself that the fault lay with the type of examination, rather than with the kind of teaching which these children had received" (p. 31). This sort of explaining is quite common today as well. When achievement scores of

American students fell in the 1980s and 1990s, one of the reactions was that the tests were at fault.

Older students experienced difficulty with writing—their style was clear and fluent but loose and inaccurate in sentence structure (p. 31).

Generally, the school tended to change over time, in the direction of the traditional, teacher-centered approach. It had originally intended to mix all ages of students so that the younger might learn from the older. But increased enrollment made this unworkable, and they went to the more traditional grouping by age. Also, they assumed originally that an "all-around teacher" would be best. This was changed to having different teachers specialize in different subjects.

No grades were originally assigned, but there were signs that some of the children wanted external marks as proof of their achievement. Also, the "ever present need to prepare the older students for their college entrance examinations" brought some grading to that group (p. 35).

With regard to the effectiveness of the broader aspects of the Laboratory School experiment—that education can be "the fundamental method of social progress and reform"—most educators concluded that no valid answers could be drawn. Indeed, historians today claim that Dewey hardly had a chance to prove or disprove his theories because of his unexpected leave from the University of Chicago and the Laboratory School to the Teachers College of Columbia University. He was, therefore, "unable to continue refining and describing the approach to educational research that he had only begun to delineate before 1904" (Lagemann, 1989, p. 202).

Noted by others as a weakness of Dewey's Laboratory School was its underestimating "the difficult problem of transforming experiments in education into sound public school practice" (Lagemann, 1989, p. 203). This criticism included the failure to provide for a curriculum that would prepare the older students for entrance into prep schools and colleges.

The foregoing reports regarding the effectiveness of the Dewey school are quite similar to those found in the quantitative research studies reported in Chapter 5. Both point to weaknesses in academic skills.

In sum, the Dewey conception of education had many enthusiastic followers among educators and lay people, but from the start there were concerns about its effectiveness in teaching reading, writing, and other academic skills. Indeed, the Laboratory School followed Dewey's philosophy that reading and writing be delayed until the child shows interest and need for these subjects. He was convinced that the skills in the fundamental subjects would come from using them for more meaningful learning. Thus, later and less formal teaching of the skill subjects was practiced. One wonders whether it was this practice that contributed to the necessity of drilling some fourteen- and fifteen-year-olds for their college entrance exams.

Overall, with time, the school seemed to become more structured, more skill-oriented, and more traditional. This could be seen from the special instruction in skills and in academic subjects made available to students preparing for college entrance exams and in grades requested by some of the children. Another sign of movement to a more traditional approach was having teachers specialize in teaching different subjects instead of the original plan of each teacher being responsible for all subjects. Although they began with all age classrooms, so that the younger children could learn from the older, they went to the more traditional grouping by age.

RUSSELL'S BEACON HILL SCHOOL

Bertrand Russell's Beacon Hill School opened in Sussex, England, in 1927 with twelve boarders and three day pupils. A strong aim of Russell's educational theory was to liberate the student's creative impulses, which would, he believed, allow the child " 'more liberty than we are accustomed to . . . although some departure from complete liberty is unavoidable if children are to be taught anything' " (Russell quotes here and below are from Hendley, 1986, p. 48). Russell acknowledged that " 'many things that must be thought about are uninteresting and even those that are interesting at first often become very wearisome before they have been considered as long as is necessary. The power of giving prolonged attention is very important and is hardly to be widely acquired except as a habit induced originally by outside pressure' " (p. 49).

Above all, argument was to be encouraged in the interest of promoting free thinking and all questions, no matter what the subject, were to be answered to the best of the teacher's knowledge and ability.

Russell further noted that absolute freedom in education would be dangerous because some children will harm themselves—drinking poison or falling out of windows. The teacher must have some authority in a way that attempts to use these natural desires and influences. His ideal scheme for education also included some specifications for an appropriate curriculum. Every child at twelve would have some instruction in classics, mathematics, and science; and by age fourteen those who wanted to would specialize. The ideal of an "all-round" education is out of date, Russell asserted: " 'it has been destroyed by the progress in knowledge' " (p. 51).

Russell noted that the ideal system of education should be divided into suitable stages that were agreeable to the average child. Thus, the right amount of freedom and discipline can be supplied so that the child will develop self-discipline. Children are not naturally good or bad, according to Russell: " 'they are born with reflexes and instincts out of which, by action of the environment, habits are produced' " (p. 53).

Other suggestions for a curriculum were to include acting, singing, dancing, and to make geography and history more interesting by use of cinema and field trips. For reading he recommended good literature, either written for adults (e.g., *Robinson Crusoe*) or written for children but also delightful to grown-ups (e.g., the works of Lewis Carroll), instead of silly sentimental books expressly written for children.

Thus, although Russell shared Dewey's goals of freedom of thought and inquiry for the child, his curriculum was geared more to the intellectual and academic, particularly for reading and writing. However, he too preferred delaying the "three Rs" until the children expressed an interest in them, but he placed this period around ages five to seven.

Overall, the ideas behind the school—the nature of children's learning and an appropriate curriculum—came from Russell's philosophy and preferences. No attempt was made to tie these ideas to research findings.

Was the Beacon Hill School a success or failure? The general impression was that it was a failure (Hendley, 1986, p. 65). One reason was poor administration. Similar to Dewey and Wirt, of the Gary schools, Russell underestimated the time and energy that would be required to run the school. Another reason for failure was that the teachers did not really believe in Russell's theory of education. According to Russell, they gave the impression that they did, but when he was not there to see what they were doing, they did what they were accustomed to doing.

Another reason for the school's failure was financial. The need for funds was so great that they admitted very difficult children who had been rejected by more conventional schools. The Russell program was not appropriate for such children, and it led to pandemonium (Hendley, 1986, p. 64).

Russell was aware of the school's mistakes:

"Young children in a group cannot be happy without a certain amount of order and routine." Left to their own devices, they will turn to bullying or other destructive behavior if only out of sheer boredom. Better to have an adult on hand to suggest activities and "to supply an initiative which is hardly to be expected of young children." (Hendley, 1986, p. 66)

The teachers had a strenuous life. They had to know their material and make it interesting enough for the students to learn it without compulsion. In addition, they had to accompany the children on hikes and supervise their meals and play. But their distress went even deeper, and was related more directly to the very principles underlying the school:

"Without a formal structure of authority to back them up, the teachers had only the strength of their own personalities to rely on in the face of children trained and encouraged to ask constant questions, to accept nothing on mere adult say-so. Those who survived and succeeded won our respect and affection; the others departed in shame and despair." (Hendley, 1986, p. 67)

Another common criticism of children educated in the Beacon Hill School was that "they did not know dull facts, e.g., irregular verbs, and that they had not the techniques for acquiring such knowledge" (p. 68).

Regarding discipline, Russell favored some routines to give students a sense of security. Routines, he believed, provided a sense of direction and discipline for the child's activities. The struggle between learning concrete facts and abstract knowledge has to be dealt with in young children. They will be interested in learning concrete facts, but they have to be compelled to gain more abstract knowledge.

Thus, Russell's Beacon Hill School, as Dewey's, became more structured over time—more interested in the need for discipline, more concerned with the learning of "dull facts." In reality, they became more traditional.

THE GARY SCHOOLS

In the early 1900s, the superintendent of the public schools in Gary, Indiana, William Wirt, initiated a form of student-centered education that spread rapidly throughout the large cities of the United States. Basing his approach on the philosophy of John Dewey, Wirt sought to make education more realistic and more suited to children growing up in an industrialized nation. The Gary system provided for different aptitudes and interests of the students and tried to prevent failure of those children who had difficulty performing in the traditional schools of the time.

Education in the Gary schools was based on active learning—learning by work and play—and designed to educate the whole child. Manual and artistic skills were not to be subordinated to the intellectual, as in most schools at that time. Wirt's plan was that "the child should have every day, in some form or another, contact with all the different activities which influence a well-rounded human being, instead of meeting them perfunctorily once or twice a week, as in the ordinary school" (Bourne, 1970, p. 15).

The Gary schools had limited finances. They were assigned only one teacher per forty students. Thus, part of the Gary plan was to have older children teaching and supervising the work and play of younger children and to make good use of school and community facilities.

The Gary school model was picked up by many cities throughout the United States. There was much excitement about these schools, particularly in the large cities. The model's grounding in the philosophy of Dewey gave Gary wide visibility. Indeed, many found in the Gary schools—as Dewey did himself—the most complete and admirable application of progressive education. The Gary plan was also praised for its better use of school buildings, libraries, and parks, and its day and evening and Saturday classes during the school year.

How well did the Gary schools achieve their objectives? Were they successful in educating a large variety of students at lower costs? Adelaine and Murray Levine, in their introduction to Bourne's book on the Gary schools, noted that visitors who came to Gary came away with the impression that they were totally successful in achieving their purposes. However, these impressions were sometimes based on rather hurried observations. Visitors came either ready to believe and overlook flaws, or they disbelieved and came prepared to find flaws (Levine & Levine, 1970).

The popularity of the Gary schools was not universal. In New York City where the Gary approach had been adopted, "smoldering resentments flared up during the latter part of October 1917 in week-long riots centered in the schools of upper Manhattan, the Bronx, and Brooklyn" (Levine & Levine, 1970, p. xli). These protests against Garyizing schools were poignantly expressed by an immigrant parent who stated: " 'We want our children to learn from books, with paper and pencils, not with sewing machines and in shops' " (Levine & Levine, 1970, p. xlii).

The intensity of the positive and negative views on the Gary schools led to a commissioned study by Abraham Flexner and Frank Bachman (1970). Flexner was famous for his study of medical education.

Flexner and Bachman had much praise for the Gary plan, particularly for its openness to new solutions for old problems. But they questioned many of its principles and practices. They were particularly concerned about the practice of having older children act as "helpers" to younger ones, frequently taking charge of classes, assisting in keeping records, correcting papers, and so on.

This practice was defended on the grounds of being educational. But, they asked, does it work? Their investigations suggested a negative answer.

Further criticism was that the Gary plan had the unrealistic expectation that it could quickly transform classroom instruction. It failed to appreciate the extreme difficulty of converting new educational principles into new educational practices—particularly in the Gary schools, where the population was largely foreign-born, where no English or very poor English was spoken, and where the staff was composed of teachers with varied training and experience.

After making allowances for some of these shortcomings, Flexner and Bachman put the blame mainly on the administration:

> Fundamentally, the defect is one of the administration. No scheme will execute itself. Precisely because the Gary scheme is complicated, extensive, and at some points novel, uncommonly watchful administrative control is requisite. Such control does not exist. In consequence, results appear to be largely taken for granted. (1970, p. 305)

Flexner and Bachman were concerned also about the confusion between standards set for the learning of skills, such as spelling and arithmetic, and those for the learning of more open and playful activities. Unfortunately, they noted, the standards appropriate for the more playful tasks were used inappropriately for the learning of academic skills.

Overall, Gary's students fell short of expected academic standards. "In reaching out for something new, Gary has too lightly parted with certain essential and established values, without being aware of the loss it has inadvertently made" (p. 307).

Flexner and Bachman were also concerned about a general lack of "workmanship" among the students. While excellent spirit was found in the playgrounds, gymnasiums, shops, laboratories, and household art departments, it was not found in academic work. Generally, standards of workmanship were lacking:

> Some boys and girls did well; some did ill. . . . Not that teachers and principals do not want good work; they plainly do. But that

patient and close attention to details by which alone good work can be obtained was far too irregular to be effective. . . . Poor spelling, arithmetical inaccuracies, and grave omissions pass unchallenged. Not only is the immediate educative effect lost, but the child tends to become habituated to inferior performance. (1970, pp. 308–309)

They conclude with praise for Gary's "trying of new things" and for making a thoughtful and intelligent attempt.

But, as with the Dewey and Russell schools, weaknesses were found in the Gary schools with regard to student learning of skills, for example, poor spelling and arithmetical inaccuracies.

A more positive view of the Gary schools is found in Ronald Cohen's *Children of the Mill* (1990). Covering the period 1906–1960, he states that the Gary schools were an example of "mass education in a multiracial, multiethnic, class-structured urban setting," providing a "plethora of services to the community, many positive, some, perhaps, negative" (p. x).

It is of interest that Cohen's thorough historical treatment of the Gary schools hardly touches on the achievement outcomes of the students—a great concern in the earlier study by Flexner (see Flexner & Bachman, 1970). Cohen writes, however, that Gary provided a wide variety of academic subjects, including "public speaking, nature study, crafts, music, manual training, athletics, and a whole host of other activities" (1990, p. xiii).

The descriptive research tends to confirm the findings from the quantitative studies. All three of the progressive, student-centered experiments experienced numerous difficulties with academic skills, standards, proficiency in writing, and the like.

CHAPTER 7

—

Student-Centered Education
From Theory to Practice

This chapter focuses on some of the ways in which student-centered educational approaches have played out in U.S. schools. How did they influence instruction and school practices, and how did they affect students' achievement levels?

As noted earlier, some researchers have found that progressive education was not as widely implemented in practice as was thought earlier. John Goodlad (1983), for example, concluded that, in spite of the strong appeal of progressive education, public schools were pretty much teaching the way they had before progressive education—paying little attention to pupil needs, attainments, and individual learning.

Cuban (1993), in his historical analysis of changes in educational theory and practice over a 100-year period, came to essentially the same conclusion. Although there has been much enthusiasm for progressive, student-centered education since the 1920s, most schools, he concluded, were following a traditional, teacher-centered approach to learning.

And yet, it would seem that most schools were influenced in some ways by progressive education. This influence was reflected by their accepting certain concepts and beliefs from progressive education without necessarily implementing the broader program.

I present below some of the beliefs and concepts from progressive education that made their way into public schools, particularly elementary schools, from the 1920s to the present. These come from my experience of fifty years in teaching, research, and consulting, my talks with teachers and administrators, my observations in hundreds of classrooms, and from the relevant educational literature. My aim is to illustrate how these beliefs and practices— which grew out of progressive education—have affected teaching and learning in public schools even when they considered themselves quite traditional.

READINESS

One of the widely accepted concepts from progressive education, particularly in elementary schools, is that of readiness—that there is a right and best time to learn based on the learner's development and interests. The concept of readiness began to influence educational thought and practice early in the 1900s, and it still has a strong influence today.

During the 1920s and 1930s, the readiness concept was popular among psychologists and educators in the teaching of reading (Gates, 1937; Morphett & Washburne, 1931). By the 1940s and 1950s most schools had accepted the idea that children learn to read best when their mental and physical development is sufficient for the task of reading. If made to learn earlier, the theory held, they become frustrated, achieve little, and ultimately turn away from reading. This idea has been accepted by traditional as well as progressive schools.

At first, the most widely used measure of readiness for learning to read was mental ability as measured by intelligence tests. Later, reading tests included measures of language development and interest in learning to read. They also included knowledge of the letters of the alphabet, hearing similarities and differences in spoken words, as well as understanding stories. Thus, the earlier definition of readiness relied on the intellectual and language abilities of the child. Later, reading tests began to rely more on skills that can be taught. Reading readiness tests were used widely to assess the beginner's ability to benefit from reading instruction.

It cannot be denied that the readiness concept that originated with child-centered educators was designed to be constructive and humane for the children. But it also created difficulties for the many whose reading instruction was delayed too long.

I recently heard about a young man who was in law school but could read only at a fifth-grade level. He was able to study law only because his mother read his law books to him. As the reason for his not having learned to read better, he explained that in school he had lacked readiness in the early grades, and so was taught to read later.

The early prediction that children with low readiness would ultimately catch up has not been adequately tested. Indeed, more recent studies of those who "lack readiness" find that proper prereading and reading instruction, rather than a delay, leads to better progress.

The effects of applying the readiness concept have been far-reaching. The tendency to delay instruction for those who find it difficult to learn in first grade has remained essentially the same, from the 1920s and 1930s until the present. What has changed is the sophistication of the explanation. From the 1930s to 1950s, it was common to say the child lacked readiness. Now the explanation tends to be more sophisticated—a modern version is that instruction in reading is not yet developmentally appropriate for the child.

I have encountered child after child in the fourth or fifth grade who is functioning on a first- or second-grade level in reading. The child is usually intellectually able, and often well above average in intelligence. The story is the same. When the child was not reading in the first grade, the parents were told not to worry. He was not quite ready. When he became ready he would learn. That usually did not happen. Instead, the child fell further behind. When he reached the fourth grade, the school called the parents for a conference and informed them that the child needs clinical assessment to find out why he has not learned.

As noted earlier, recent research, as well as some of the old research, finds that readiness can be developed (Gates, 1937). Thus, the readiness concept, which delays learning until the child is ready, may not be optimal for the child's development. In most instances earlier rather than later learning leads to higher achievement in later grades, and earlier attention to the "lack of readiness" leads to better progress than waiting for readiness.

STUDENT CHOICE

Another concept from progressive education that made its way into large numbers of public schools—whether traditional or progressive—is that students learn best if they choose what they want to learn, when they want to learn it, and what pace suits them best.

In a recent discussion with a Head Start director in Michigan, I was informed, with much pride, that their four-year-olds choose what they want to do. This, the director noted, was based on Piaget's theories of child development. Yet, he had little to say about the children's choices and what is to be done with their choices. What seemed to be more important to the director was that each child had an opportunity to choose. What the child was expected to learn from his or her choices seemed of less importance. The preschool program was viewed mainly as giving the children freedom to choose—to be freed from outer constraints.

Why is choice so important for four-year-olds? Is it that a planned instructional program might be considered too traditional or too structured?

Early childhood education in America has had a strong concern for freedom and openness and less concern for academic learning. Early childhood educators were perhaps among the first romantics. And they still tend to view the education of preschoolers as an opportunity for enhancing mainly social and emotional development, with the child's intellectual development seemingly judged to be less important. Indeed, preschool education has long been concerned that there not be too early an emphasis on academic learning (see Hall, 1901).

More recently, there seems to be a growing interest in teacher-directed learning for very young children. One hears from time to time of proposals to teach the young about the dangers of alcohol and drugs, starting at age three or maybe even two. Are we perhaps preparing ourselves for a return to a more didactic approach to learning?

Freedom of choice has also been an ideal condition in the elementary school since about the 1920s among teachers and administrators. The most praised reading programs from the 1920s to the present have relied on self-selection of books. Of course, not all elementary school teachers have been able to do "the ideal" thing. Most have relied on published reading programs that do not permit as much student choice. But often one finds these teachers apologizing that having a large class, many students with problems, and many students who have difficulty learning makes it hard for them to give the children more choice.

The theory behind student choice holds that learning is most effective when it is under the control of the learners themselves. What to learn, when to learn, and how to learn should, according to this theory, come from the learner, not from the teacher.

And yet the research finds that the students do less well academically when they are given freedom to choose, select, and pace their own learning (see Chapter 5; see also Barth, 1972; Chall & Curtis, 1991; Chall, Jacobs, & Baldwin, 1990; and Chall & Peterson, 1986).

Teacher-centered learning is particularly effective for those who enter school with limited knowledge, language, experience, and skills. They have not had the opportunity to learn some of the beginning skills in reading, writing, and mathematics that progressive, student-centered approaches tend to assume comes naturally and that the upper- and middle-class child usually acquires at home. When children fail to learn in a student-centered school environment, the explanation usually is that they lack maturity or readiness. And yet their lack is often just the failure to receive the necessary instruction.

There has been such strong belief in the progressive ideal of student centered learning that schools have tended to give too little attention to seeking out the best instructional procedures. Instead, they have tended to look to the strengths and weaknesses of the children for explanations of learning. The scenario is fairly predictable. We stimulate the children to learn. We try to keep them happy and creative, and we build their self-esteem. We give them choice: they are given freedom to select what interests them and when they will learn. This will result in their desire to learn and in their interest in learning—or so goes the script.

Since some children do fall behind, even with self-selection and student-centered learning, how is this explained? First, it is explained in terms of the child's abilities and disabilities. During the past decade, attention to the child's learning style has been proposed as a means of preventing learning problems. By administering various tests, the teacher is able to assess the child's learning style and can then select the methods that go with that style.

Failure to succeed is also explained in terms of the child's needing extra time to develop the readiness needed. If progress is not made in academic subjects, the school looks to other, deeper causes or emphasizes the child's other talents, for example, his or her talent in art or citizenship.

Usually the teacher begins to worry about academic learning when the child is manifesting psychological problems—is too aggressive, or too submissive, or resists activities related to reading and writing. It is then that a referral is usually made to an educational specialist or to a psychiatrist or psychologist.

TEACHING THE WHOLE CHILD
AND MAKING SCHOOL A HAPPY PLACE

Since the 1920s the ideal goal of education, particularly elementary education, has been to educate the whole child—and a happy child. This concept originated with the child-centered reformers, but it became widely accepted, in principal at least, by all kinds of schools—teacher-centered as well as student centered.

The widely held concern for keeping the child happy and interested often led to concern for entertaining the child (Hersey, 1954). The most widely used reading series in the United States listed as its first objective—first out of thirty-six—"to create a feeling of pleasure and satisfaction from reading humorous, surprising, and interesting stories" (p. 137). The twenty-first objective was "to develop the ability to read short sentences with understanding, both orally and silently."

Is it not misplaced emphasis, to say the least, when the objective of deriving pleasure from an act is put so far ahead of the objective of learning to perform the act? Is not the point that pleasure in itself is not an objective of the school curriculum at all, that learning is the main objective, and that pleasure may be an aid, a motivation, a means toward the realization of the true objective and a wonderfully desirable by-product of its attainment? (Hersey, 1954, p. 137)

This misplaced emphasis is still a problem in beginning reading. Whole language, the current student-centered approach to beginning reading, also places the first emphasis not on learning to read but rather on the reading of "authentic" literature, right from the start, that is interesting and enjoyable to the reader. During the 1990s there has also been a tendency to put "self-esteem" as the first objective of learning in place of academic learning itself.

THE CONCEPT OF WHOLENESS AND NATURALNESS

Since the advent of progressive education, wholeness has been the ideal of many schools. There has been concern for the whole child, not just for the child's intellect, but for his or her social and emotional development. This concept has been applied to the curriculum, as well. Educators, whether progressive or traditional have tended to speak not of reading, writing, spelling, grammar, and so on, but rather of the "language arts."

The ideal has also been to foster natural learning, which comes from the needs of the individual, not from the wishes of the teacher or the school. Accordingly, learning should come from intrinsic motivation, not from outward incentives and rewards.

Learning should be free, natural, and at the learner's own pace. Children have an inner desire to learn, and teachers should surround them with the materials from which they can learn and should free them to do the learning. Therefore, readiness is all. If children are not ready, they will not learn. To teach before the child is ready may be harmful.

The ideal in which learning is viewed as natural or organic—

preferred by progressive educators since the early 1900s—has gradually made its way into the public schools. Nevertheless, educators have been able to maintain some external standards through their use of textbooks, workbooks, computer software, and standardized achievement tests.

INDIVIDUAL DIFFERENCES

The progressive concept of individual differences—that in any given classroom there is a wide range of talent and achievement, and that teachers should take each pupil at his or her best learning pace—has also made its way into teacher-centered schools, as well as student-centered. Among its weak features is that although assessment of individual differences may be met for reading instruction, they are not easily met for content subjects. Even if a fourth-grade student receives reading instruction at a second-grade level, he is expected to use a fourth-grade social studies text when learning social studies.

A typical example of the dilemma is as follows: The mother of a fourth grader visited the fourth grader's teacher to express her horror at finding that her son was unable to read the arithmetic problems he had been given for homework, and insisted that the teacher bring him up to his grade level as soon as possible. The teacher claimed that she had been helping him but he was, after all, one of thirty pupils. She had followed the third-grade teacher's policy of teaching him "at his level" (Hersey, 1954, p. 140).

Another weak feature of the concept of individual levels is the difficulties they pose for the teacher. To cope with this challenge, teachers focus their teaching on students who lag behind, while advanced students are seldom given more challenging work. They are instead given "enrichment" at their grade level (i.e., broader work at the same grade level). I found similar practices in classrooms I visited in the middle 1960s for my study *Learning to Read: The Great Debate* (Chall, 1967, 1983a, 1996a).

The concept of individual differences is one of the most humane concepts of the new education. Yet, it can easily become one of the most destructive. Unless it is clear to all—to administrators, teachers, students, and parents—that standards need to be met at given ages and grades for students of different abilities, and that those who do not meet these standards are to be given additional instruction, we will have a greater number of students lagging further and further behind as they proceed through school. If students who lag behind are not given the additional instruction they need to continue to make progress, they will fall further and further behind at each successive grade. If teachers accept the student's low achievement as a manifestation of individual differences, the deceleration in achievement in later grades becomes ever greater. When such students reach high school, they usually are placed in special classes that are less challenging academically. Many drop out of school with minimal achievement. If they do manage to complete high school and enter a community college, they will need to take remedial courses in reading, writing, and math. The average reading ability of freshmen in typical two-year colleges is about the eighth-grade level instead of the expected thirteenth-grade level (Mullis et al., 1993).

SOCIAL PROMOTION

The concept of social promotion—promotion to the next grade irrespective of achievement–has been popular from the early 1920s onwards. It has been an almost universal concept in U.S. educational circles and has been based on the psychological findings that children grow and develop at different rates and, therefore, cannot be expected to learn at the same pace.

Individual differences were originally assessed by differences in verbal intelligence. More recently the concept began to include differences in socioeconomic status, social and emotional factors, and neurological differences. Many teachers began to accept lower standards from students who were seen as having problems and tried to adjust the instruction to their abilities. The students were usually taught on a level below that expected of most students in their class—not because their teachers did not care but because they often cared too much. They did not wish to hurt the students more than they were already hurt.

When the lag became very great, the schools tended to call in experts from fields other than education—psychologists, sociologists, linguists, neurologists, and psychiatrists—to suggest solutions. In spite of well-established evidence from research and practice that good instruction is the most effective treatment for those who lag behind and that learning is itself therapeutic, schools sought out causes and solutions of poor achievement that often were based on therapy, not instruction.

Social promotion has also meant that the teacher, in grades beyond the first or second, has the difficult task of teaching a class with students who vary widely in achievement. This variation grows with each successive grade and becomes more onerous for the teacher.

Social promotion has been viewed as a humane alternative to the traditional practice of "holding back" those who lag behind in achievement. More recently, the large numbers of students who lag behind their grade placement has brought back an interest in doing away with social promotion. Many call for promoting students only if they "catch up" in summer school or through tutoring.

GROUPING

One solution, particularly for the first few grades, has been to group the children by achievement within each class. This approach was considered a more humane and democratic way of adjusting to individual differences than the earlier whole-class teaching of the traditional school. Indeed, in the early 1950s when I supervised student teachers, we rated whole-class teaching as less acceptable than teaching small groups that varied in ability.

During the 1950s, one of my graduate students at the City College did a master's thesis on the attitudes of third graders toward grouping for reading instruction. Did they like it? She found that only those in the most advanced group liked it. Those in the middle group liked it somewhat. Those in the lowest group disliked it very much, but they would like it, they said, if they were in the highest group.

After about five decades of viewing within-class grouping by achievement as the most democratic and humane solution to individual differences, shortcomings began to be expressed. John Goodlad came forth with perhaps the most devastating criticism. In his studies of elementary school classes, he found that children who were in the lowest group in the first grade tended also to be in the lowest group in the upper grades.

From the best evidence available it would appear that a return to holding all students in each grade to average standards could be disastrous—unless special help is given to those who lag behind. It could result in having fourteen-year-olds sitting in classes with nine-year-olds. This situation could lead to feelings of shame and failure for the children who are "left back." What seems to work best is a good instructional program for all children. For those who are achieving on a level below their grade, special remedial instruction should also be provided.

DROPOUTS

Student-centered concepts have also tended to dominate our explanations of why students drop out of school. The individual's social and psychological problems have been favored as reasons in spite of research findings that dropping out is highly related to low achievement. It is not that low achievement was overlooked entirely as a cause for dropping out. But it seemed to be considered of lesser importance than nonschool factors such as socioeconomic status, education of parents, minority status, ethnicity, and the like.

Why do we tend to seek "deeper" underlying psychological and sociological causes of dropping out of school? It is quite reasonable to expect students to drop out when they know they are failing. It is painful to keep exposing oneself to continued failure. And it must be deeply humiliating to a high school student to have the teacher read the textbook to the class because they are not able to read it themselves—or to have the teacher rewrite parts of the textbook so that it can be read by the students. Why, they may ask, did no one in the school take them aside and teach them to read and write long before they got to high school? Or send them to a school that could do it?

Recently, Jencks and Phillips have revised their earlier position regarding the major impact of socioeconomic factors on achievement. They now conclude—on the basis of more recent data—that school factors are the strongest predictors of achievement and test performance, especially among those students whose achievement is low (Jencks & Phillips, 1998).

LESS RELIANCE ON TEXTBOOKS, WORKBOOKS, AND HOMEWORK

Student-centered education early on played down the importance of textbooks, workbooks, and homework and put greater emphasis on experience, field trips, and literature. These preferences were also adopted by teacher-centered schools.

A mother who was born and educated in France told me recently that, when her young daughter was in the second grade in a U.S. public school, she went to see the teacher to introduce herself and to express her willingness to cooperate in seeing that the child's homework was done as the teacher wished. The teacher responded sternly, "We don't give homework—we believe that children should enjoy themselves." And so, with these few words, the teacher informed the mother about the practice of American education.

DISCOVERY LEARNING AND PROBLEM SOLVING VERSUS KNOWLEDGE AND SKILLS

One of the persistent debates between student- and teacher-centered education has been whether the major emphasis of instruction should be on knowledge and skills or on the higher mental processes—the ability to think, solve problems, and create. In reality, both teacher-centered and student-centered teachers consider creativity and problem solving to be the ultimate outcomes of education. But they generally believe there are different ways to get there.

The difference seems to lie in the emphasis and timing that each places on acquiring skills and knowledge and their place in problem solving. Beginning with Dewey, student-centered educators have tended to place less importance on acquiring knowledge and skills—on the assumption that these are acquired naturally from an emphasis on problem solving. Teacher-centered educators tend to place greater importance on acquiring knowledge because they believe it is needed in problem solving. Student-centered educators favor problem solving from the start. Some, in fact, fear that, if problem-solving experiences are delayed too long, students will be limited in their ability to solve problems. Teacher-centered educators, on the other hand, tend to favor starting with basic skills and knowledge, then proceeding to problem solving.

As we saw earlier, the new math of the 1960s sought to raise achievement by focusing on problem solving and the use of higher mental processes from the start. Even the youngest students were taught to think like mathematicians, with less emphasis on computation. By the early 1970s, a strong reaction against the new math set in, with claims that children's computation skills had been weakened.

Changes in the teaching of reading parallel those in the teaching of math. The new reading of the 1930s to the 1960s, as well as the new reading of the 1980s and 1990s, also stressed higher mental processes from the start. The assumption was that when emphasis is placed, from the beginning, on the meaning of what is read, the ability to recognize and decode words in print would be acquired more rapidly.

The new math and the new reading relied on the learners' "discovering" the skills—computation for math and word recognition and phonics (the alphabetic principle) for reading. They assumed that "basics" come naturally from an emphasis on the higher mental processes. But as we saw earlier, this assumption has not been borne out by research or in practice (see Chapter 4). What the research has found is that those who learn the basics early in school do better in reading and math—on tests of basic skills and ultimately in problem solving. Progress in higher-level cognitive skills—problem solving in math and comprehension in reading—is usually slowed down when basic skills are not automatic (see Chall, 1967, 1983a, 1996a).

Although the supporting research on these questions has been available for nearly a century, little attention has been paid to it. Instead, the ideal position since the early 1900s has been to develop in students broad meanings and problem-solving ability rather than skills, facts, and knowledge.

It is important to note that these student-centered concepts have been the ideal in most American public schools since about the early 1900s. They have been taught in teachers' colleges, in workshops for teachers, and in methods textbooks for prospective teachers. They have been incorporated in student textbooks and in the teachers' manuals that accompany them. And a growing number of institutes sponsored by colleges, professional societies, publishers, and other educational groups have helped disseminate these ideals.

Beginning in the late 1980s there were several calls for a greater emphasis on the acquisition of knowledge. E. D. Hirsch (1987, 1996) called for a greater focus on knowledge in the elementary school, while Allan Bloom (1987) called for a more rigorous collegiate education. Essentially, both argued for a return to a greater emphasis on knowledge and on the learning of content. Both agreed that we need aspects of the new education— but that we must not give up what works best in the old education, either.

Research on the greater effectiveness for achievement of the early acquisition of reading skills has been available at least since the 1920s (see Chall, 1967). Further, aspects of reading and vocabulary have been found to influence higher verbal functioning. Thus, J. B. Carroll noted that low scores on the analogies subtest of the SAT stemmed not only from difficulty with analogies but more commonly from a limited vocabulary—that is, many who had difficulty with analogies did not know the meanings of the words used in the analogies (J. B. Carroll, personal communication, 1977).

In an analysis of the NAEP reading tests, Curtis (1986) found that many test items classified as measuring higher-level thought processes were actually measuring lower-level skills, and that "even at higher levels of reading, lower level skills still remain a critical component of reading" (p. 6).

The recognition that we have been moving from a manufacturing- to a knowledge-based economy has brought even greater realization that more students will need to know how to solve problems in their work. The need to think and understand is even greater today than it was in Dewey's time. The growth of science and technology has also led to a focus on thinking rather than on knowing. This has brought a passionate plea for the teaching of understanding and problem solving from the early grades onward (see Chapter 2, pages 23–25; Elmore, (1995); Gardner & Boix-Mansilla, 1994; Resnick et al., 1989). At the same time, we cannot assume that the learning of skills and knowledge is *less* essential, since the research indicates that higher learning depends heavily on both.

THE TEACHER AS FACILITATOR

Before the 1920s there seemed to be agreement among U.S. educators that the role of teachers was to teach. With the growth of progressive, student-centered education, the teacher's role has become less clear. Indeed, there has been a growing tendency to no longer regard the role of teaching as the major objective of teachers. Increasingly, even how we refer to teachers has changed. As school directories demonstrate, many teachers are now called facilitators, coaches, or resource persons.

The ideal, student-centered teacher is one who encourages and sets the stage for student learning, but does not do direct teaching. While "less teaching" may contribute to independence among some students and enhance the learning of able students, it puts greater strain on students who are less able. Indeed, the research reported in Chapter 5 confirms that direct instruction has a beneficial effect particularly on those whose learning is less proficient. The student-centered ideal that "the less the teacher teaches, the better the students learn" often has negative consequences, especially among those who have difficulty in learning. It may well lead to the greater number of poor achievers in U.S. schools, as compared to Japanese schools in which strong instruction by teachers is the ideal (Stevenson & Stigler, 1992).

Even in more teacher-centered U.S. schools, teachers have also become relatively less involved in teaching. With the greater participation of other professionals in the children's learning—psychologists, language therapists, remedial reading specialists, volunteer tutors, parents, and special educators—the teacher's time devoted to teaching has lessened, the result being that even these teachers are increasingly resembling student-centered teachers.

PARENTS AS TEACHERS

As the role of the teacher as teacher has declined, parents are expected to take on some of the work of teaching. They are expected to read to their children before kindergarten, to engage in language games, and generally to prepare them for school. For those children already in school, parents are expected to help with homework and projects and to read *with* them. Indeed, one of the growing popular explanations for children's slow progress in reading and writing is that their parents have not read to and with them or helped them enough in other ways.

The social-cultural and ethnic background of parents is used increasingly to explain a child's academic achievement or lack of it. Of course, it has been known from as early as the 1700s that family background is related to school achievement (Eppenstein, 1966). Strong evidence was published for the importance of family influences thirty-five years ago in James Coleman's *Equality of Educational Opportunity in the United States* (1966). One of the most comprehensive studies of school achievement, and one of the most widely read at the time, it concluded that the most potent factor in a child's achievement was the parents' socioeconomic status—not the money spent per child by the school he or she attended, or the instruction received (see Chapter 8, pages 142–144, for more detail on the Coleman study and its effects).

Other studies conducted at about the same time reported similar results—that the causes of poor achievement lay mainly in the social and cultural background and education of parents. There were, of course, studies that found schooling and teaching did make a difference (see Chapter 5), but they received less attention. Overall, faith in the schools' ability to improve student achievement seemed to have declined with the publication of studies that found stronger effects for economic and cultural factors. This feeling was detectable in the remark of an early childhood teacher in the 1980s: "I tell my children, just as their parents go off to work, school is their work. Am I wrong in this?" Earlier, in the summer of 1954, in a class on the teaching of reading, an outstanding first-grade teacher said: "My children all tested below average in reading readiness. But I taught them to read. Did I do wrong?" I wondered then, as I wonder now, why teachers so often fear that they do wrong when they teach. Is it the power of the student-centered concept that they must not frustrate their students with work that is too demanding? Has the student-centered emphasis on experience, creativity, and enjoyment spread to teacher-centered schools?

It should be noted that the preference for experience and enjoyment stems also from various developments in the culture—the influence of television, computer games, and popular youth culture. Student-centered schools were only one (albeit a major one) of the many influences contributing to the belief that students should have fun while learning.

SELF-ESTEEM

Teacher-centered education views self-esteem as an outcome of doing what one does, especially when one does it well. Student-centered education tends to take a different view, namely, that self-esteem is a prerequisite for learning. This view has a long history, probably receiving its earliest support from the theories of Freud and other psychologists who held that emotional problems were the cause of much poor school achievement (Chall & Peterson, 1986).

Recently, using the concept of self-esteem to explain why students learn or do not learn has spread to all kinds of schools, traditional as well as progressive. Thus, when children fail, lack of self-esteem is often cited. The result in such instances is that certain teaching procedures become favored because they are presumed to raise student self-esteem. We hear more and more that certain practices, such as hands-on science, are worthwhile because they also enhance students' self-esteem. One hears of schools whose first objective is to build students' self-esteem, hoping it will bring about improved academic achievement.

While one can appreciate that self-esteem is a worthy goal in itself, a considerable amount of research and past experience suggests that pursuing it as a means of raising achievement levels will be an incomplete solution, at best. American children, according to Stevenson and Stigler (1992), already have higher self-esteem than Asian children, but they manifest much lower achievement. Indeed, they wrote, American children as a whole may well have too much self-esteem.

Is it self-esteem that students lack, or is it that they lack interest in academic learning? Julian Stanley of Johns Hopkins University, who directed a special program for elementary and high school students talented in mathematics, found that many students invited to join advanced math classes opted not to accept the offer (personal communication, 1987). Moreover, their parents agreed with their choice. The parents worried that advanced work in mathematics (particularly in elementary school) would make their children seem different from their peers. Parents (naturally) want their children to be "normal," "all-around," "well-adjusted" persons. Many feared that learning advanced mathematics in elementary school would stand in the way of their child's social development.

WHEN STUDENTS FAIL:
PREVENTION VERSUS TREATMENT

Schools following the student-centered pattern have tended to try to adapt the methods and materials normally used to students who have difficulty learning. Indeed, since the early 1900s teachers have been encouraged to adjust the curriculum to students' abilities and interests by individualizing instruction or through small-group instruction. There has also been a growing concern among some teachers for adjusting to each student's individual learning style, for example, whether primarily by ear or by eye.

Usually those who favor a teacher-centered educational approach have sought methods and materials that would be optimal for the entire class—or most of the class—that is, those making good progress as well as those lagging behind. Their focus has also been more on preventing learning difficulties than on treating them with special procedures when found.

Indeed, as noted earlier, the preference for differentiating instruction as a means of improving learning has been one of the strong features of the student-centered pattern—and it appears to have become an ideal. Teachers are expected to give instruction through grouping by ability in the same classroom, and increasingly they are urged to adjust instruction to each student's learning style. With so much differentiated instruction going on in large classes, it should not be difficult to calculate that each child will receive only a few minutes of individualized instruction each day.

Why have we tended to put relatively less effort into finding methods and procedures that are most effective in reducing the number of students who fail? Why do we seem to put more faith in correcting problems once they are encountered? There are, no doubt, many reasons. The first is that it is hard to find procedures that will work for children with different strengths and weaknesses. But such procedures do exist. A second reason is that the student-centered concept of individualization has been generally accepted as the ideal mode of instruction. Most teachers and administrators see individual instruction as the ideal, although it is probably difficult to implement well in a classroom.

Some forms of prevention have, of course, been tried. During the 1970s early diagnosis was recommended for four- and five-year-olds who were predicted to have difficulty in learning to read. Those who showed signs of having difficulty were to be given special instruction in transition classes that would prepare them for learning in regular first-grade classes (Jansky & de Hirsch, 1972). This approach turned out to be quite difficult to carry out, and it was expensive. Moreover, Shepard (1989) found that at-risk children who attended regular classes without transition classes did better than those who had attended the transition classes. Further study revealed that instruction was more rigorous in the regular classes for these lower-achieving children than it was in the transition classes.

It is of interest that Asian schools, which are not as concerned as we are with individual differences, tend to do better with low-achieving students than we do (Stevenson & Stigler, 1992). They tend to have all children in a class work together, as we did in the United States prior to the 1920s. Methods that worked best with most students were used along with extra help given by the teacher to those who needed it.

We have tried, ideally, to adjust the curriculum to the level of achievement of different learners rather than designing programs that work well for most of them—the low as well as the high achievers—giving extra help to those who need it. Reading Recovery is a remedial program designed to prevent continued reading failure by providing individual reading instruction in the first grade for those who are lagging; but it is still mainly a one-to-one treatment program rather than a prevention program, for it has not adapted its techniques to teach regular first graders as a means of preventing failure.

SELECTING INSTRUCTIONAL MATERIALS

Teacher-centered classes have traditionally been assigned textbooks and other instructional materials by the school or district. Since student-centered teachers are expected to adjust learning to their students' abilities and interests, one might expect that they would be given greater freedom to select the instructional materials for their classes. In actuality, little choice is given to teachers except perhaps in the choice of supplementary materials or serving on a committee to select the textbooks for their grade, in their school or district. Choice of materials comes, instead, from researchers, curriculum specialists, and administrators. This approach opens the schools to hard sells from these groups, and particularly from educational publishers.

A few years ago on public television a panel of educators discussed a new reading test. I cite this panel discussion because it provides many insights into how decisions are made regarding the purchase and use of educational materials. Several of these educators gave the test their warm praise. One of the panelists, a school administrator, noted that teachers are "held hostage to materials. . . . They are made to use specific books and specific pages. Therefore they can't do real teaching. Teachers aren't allowed to have input in developing a curriculum."

Many of the comments were concerned with the student-centered quest for matching the curriculum to the individual needs of students. Panelists expressed frustration about the difficulty of selecting materials appropriate for students of such diverse achievement levels.

Perhaps it was because the panelists were communicating with parents and other nonprofessionals that their comments did not refer to any research findings. They seemed, instead, to base their comments solely on their own experiences and observations.

WHERE IS THE RESEARCH EVIDENCE?

The tendency to show little concern for evidence of success is quite common in the schools. I observed this when, in the early 1990s, I was invited to meet with teachers in an elementary school in

Maine. Hostility had broken out between the teachers who favored the new literature-based, whole language reading approach and those who wished to continue to use the traditional reading methods that they had been using with very good results. But that previous success did not satisfy those who favored whole language. They kept after the teachers who wished to teach in a more traditional manner. After a year of battling, the teachers who had preferred to use the more traditional methods said they would "give in" if they were taught how to use the new method.

The irony in this story is that the new literature-based, approach was already producing poorer results on standardized reading tests in that particular school. Other schools were also reporting poor results with the literature based program.

New programs tend to be given a hard sell when they are first proposed. The ideas are presented at professional conferences, institutes, workshops, university classes, school systems, and educational publishing houses, which display and demonstrate the materials representing the new methods—although the research evidence of their superiority is not made available.

When these new approaches do not produce the expected gains, the common explanation is that teachers have not received appropriate and sufficient instruction in their use (see Honig, 1996). Also, the complaint is voiced that the tests used to assess the new methods do not really assess the appropriately, *important* outcomes.

There is a strong tendency to seek consensus. Thus, in spite of the student-centered concept that methods and materials should suit the individual student, there is great pressure on all teachers to use whole language even if it may not suit all children. There is often a tendency to follow an "all or nothing" kind of thinking about instruction. If literature is good, then anything that is not literature is inappropriate. If individualized reading is regarded as good, then whole-class reading is held in lesser regard.

Much effort goes into winning acceptance for the new methods and materials. The new method becomes the true method, and it cannot be questioned even though its weaknesses may be found quite early. Instead, it seems to take on an "all or none" position that is strenuously debated. This makes it difficult to look objectively even at the good features of the opposing view.

SUMMARY

I have attempted to show that many of the educational ideas and practices that have been proposed and implemented since the early 1900s by practitioners of the new student-centered education were later accepted by the more traditional public schools. Most of the new ideas and practices were designed to make the life of the child more democratic, humane, and joyful. It was assumed that these approaches would lead to improved, richer, more enduring, and useful learning. When the effects of these new ideas and practices are examined closely, however, it is found (as with all great revolutionary movements) that (despite the creators' best intentions) weaknesses and difficulties have arisen. Indeed, some of these new ideas and practices may have brought about problems as great or greater than the practices and ideas they were designed to replace.

CHAPTER 8

Socioeconomic and Learning Difference Effects

For at least two centuries socioeconomic status has been recognized as an essential factor in how well students learn and achieve in school. As far back as the eighteenth century certain educational methods were praised because they worked as well with poor children as they did with rich children (Eppenstein, 1966).

During the 1920s and 1930s, many educators were concerned that student-centered education would be less effective with poor than with rich children. At that time, an Italian working-class resident of Greenwich Village in New York City put it this way, in discussing a local student-centered experiment:

> "The program of that school is suited to the children of well-to-do homes, not to our children. We send our children to school for what we cannot give them ourselves, grammar and drill. The Fifth Avenue children learn to speak well in their homes. We do not send our children to school for group activity; they get plenty of that in the street. But the Fifth Avenue children are lonely. I can see how group experience is an important form of education for them." (quoted in Cremin, 1961, p. 212)

That student-centered education may not be geared to the needs of poor children is still not resolved, even today. The writings of Lisa Delpit are particularly relevant to this question. Two articles of hers in *The Harvard Educational Review* (1986, 1988) make a poignant plea for traditional educational practices for poor African American children. While student-centered education works for white children, she notes, it does not work for poor African American children.

Delpit, an African American, attended Catholic schools as a child and youth, where she was exposed to a traditional, teacher-centered education. She was introduced to the values of student-centered education when she attended the graduate school of education of a prestigious eastern university.

Delpit vividly contrasts the two approaches. She notes that her graduate school education advocated that a new dialect is most effectively acquired indirectly, not directly by being corrected. Yet, the "poor Black Catholic school that I attended corrected every other word I uttered in their effort to coerce my Black English into sometimes hypercorrect Standard English forms acceptable to Black nuns in Catholic schools. Yet, I learned to speak and write in Standard English" (Delpit, 1986, p. 37).

Her graduate studies also advocated that learning to write is best done in a meaningful context, not by learning skills and grammar, and that "open education was the most 'humanizing' of learning environments, that children should be in control of their own learning, and that all children would read when they were ready" (1986, p. 38). Delpit applied these open education principles in her own classroom. The other, mostly older black teachers "focused on 'skills,' they made students sit down at desks, they made students practice handwriting, they corrected oral and written grammar" (1986, p. 38). Delpit threw out the desks in her classroom and provided only open learning areas with "learning stations." She had children "write books and stories to share; [and] provided games and used weaving to teach math and fine motor skills" (1986, p. 38). In the end, she said that the methods worked for some children. "My White children zoomed ahead. . . . They did amazing things with books and writing. My Black students . . . learned how to weave; and they threw the books around the learning stations" (1986, p. 38).

What was the problem? Delpit found that it was the student-centered classroom itself. She then turned to more traditional approaches. "As my classroom became more 'traditional' . . . it seemed that my Black students steadily improved in their reading and writing. But they still lagged behind," and "I still felt that I had failed in the task that was most important to me—teaching Black children and teaching them well. . . . At least I did not fall into the trap of talking about the parents' failures" (1986, p. 38).

For writing, the student-centered education preference was for focusing on "holistic" processes with an emphasis on "fluency" and creative expression, not on "correctness" or "skills," which open educators claimed "would stifle students' writing" (1986, p. 39). Delpit changed her teaching of writing after she attended a conference where she met an old friend, a teacher in an alternative school. This teacher insisted that process writing was doing " 'a monumental disservice to Black children.' " She said, " 'Our kids *are* fluent. What they need are the skills that will get them into college. I've got a kid right now—brilliant. But he can't get a score on the SAT that will even get him considered by any halfway decent college. He needs *skills*, not *fluency*' " (1986, p. 39).

Delpit was troubled that people she respected had such different views on the matter. Indeed, she was aware of taking a "great risk" when she moved toward a teacher-centered emphasis. She feared being misunderstood, and she feared that a more traditional method might subject black and other minority children to isolated, meaningless drills.

> I certainly do not suggest that the writing-process approach to literacy development is wrong or that a completely skills-oriented program is right. I suggest, instead, that there is much to be gained from the interaction of the two orientations and that advocates of both approaches have something to say to each other. (1986, p. 41)

The suggestion by Delpit that teachers "combine" the best of both educational patterns has been repeated by educators for about 100 years. Even Dewey, who was one of the most eloquent critics of traditional education, recommended from time to time that teachers not give up completely on the teaching of skills and knowledge. And even the most severe of critics of progressive, student-centered education have reminded teachers that, in the final analysis, education is for problem solving as well as for learning skills and acquiring knowledge.

Why, one may ask, do these cautionary pleas get lost? This is perhaps one of the most important questions in education in the United States. Why indeed can't we be reasonable and take the best of each approach? Perhaps the answer is that our current teacher education regimen does not provide sufficiently deep understanding of both approaches to enable teachers to self-select the best of each approach. But I think the problem is more complex than that. My analysis of the two basic approaches shows that their differences are more than just methodological. Teacher- and student-centered programs differ in their philosophy, psychology, and often in their politics. Indeed, Delpit's move from open education to more traditional ways of teaching was not easy for her. She describes her great anguish as she left behind many of the progressive ways she had learned in her graduate school days. It is of interest that she did not say what she did to combine them. (See also Jackson, 1986, for differences between the approaches.)

Delpit's second article (1988), written two years later, was largely a response to the concerns raised by the 1986 article. It focused more on the political and cultural differences of black, minority, and poor children as compared to mainstream whites. But it also elaborated further on the main theme of the earlier article, namely, that black children need a greater emphasis on direct instruction and skills than do white children, and that progressive, student-centered education does not provide it. Delpit also is more conciliatory about the two approaches used together, noting that skillful teachers use both. Her position is stated quite clearly:

> Those who are most skillful at educating Black and poor children do not allow themselves to be placed in "skills" or "process" boxes. They understand the need for both approaches, the need to help students to establish their own voices, but to coach those voices to produce notes that will be heard clearly in the larger society. (1988, p. 53)

But Delpit seemed to suffer from her decision to put a greater focus on skills and traditional teaching. She expressed a sense of isolation as she moved from an open, student-centered to a more traditional way of teaching. She expressed fear of losing her friends, her fellow teachers, and the respect of her professors because she no longer shared their optimism about the superiority of student-centered education.

Others have expressed similar views to Delpit's. In January 1977 the *Phi Delta Kappan* carried an article by Jesse Jackson on his PUSH for Excellence program, a movement for academic excellence through hard work. The article quoted Jackson as saying that the reason black children do not do well in school is that they don't practice enough. If they practiced their school work as they practiced basketball and other sports, they would be excellent in academic work as well. Jackson called for a return to a more traditional education for black children, one that required hard work and concentration (Jackson, 1977). A couple of years later, Ron Edmonds, an African American educator, took a similar position in advocating a more traditional, teacher-centered education for poor black children (see Edmonds, 1979).

Although others had come to essentially the same conclusion—that the direct teaching of skills is better for poor black children than an open, student-centered emphasis—Delpit presents her case in a highly personal manner, without reference to earlier studies. A recent book by Delpit, *Other People's Children: Cultural Conflict in the Classroom* (1995), contains the two essays from the *Harvard Educational Review* discussed here as well as an essay on ways of using the language and culture children bring with them from home. She also includes suggestions for teaching literacy to at-risk students.

Various studies during the 1970s and 1980s (many treated at greater length in Chapter 5) concluded much the same as Delpit did, namely, that for low-income students (regardless of race) a more traditional, teacher-centered education results in better achievement than a progressive, student-centered education.

George Weber (1971) identified and studied four inner-city schools whose predominantly poor and nonwhite third graders were achieving well in reading. Specifically, they were reading at or above average levels nationwide, and these schools also had an unusually low number of nonreaders. The reading scores in these schools were comparable to those in average-income schools and were markedly higher than average scores in low-income schools.

Weber found that the high reading achievement in these schools was related to eight factors: "strong leadership, high expectations, good atmosphere, strong emphasis on reading, additional reading personnel, use of phonics, individualization, and careful evaluation of student progress" (1971, p. 26). With the possible exception of "individualization," all of these factors are hallmarks of traditional, teacher-centered schools. Indeed, Weber's comments make even clearer the effectiveness of the traditional characteristics for success. He notes that it is

> difficult to escape the conviction that the order, sense of purpose, relative quiet, and pleasure in learning in these schools play a role in their achievements. Disorder, noise, tension, and confusion are found in many inner-city schools at the elementary level. . . . The four successful schools were quite different. . . .
>
> In these days of television, of many new media in the schools, and of a widespread interest in the "affective" side of learning, in many inner-city schools reading seems to be only one subject among many . . . [while in the four successful schools] reading is the first concern of the primary grades. (Weber, 1971, pp. 26–27)

Weber was particularly impressed with the "order and purpose of a well-run school" (1971, p. 15). Daily homework was given at all levels, and the early reading program was well planned, uniform, and highly structured, following a kindergarten program involving "acquisition of fundamental knowledge and concepts" (p. 6).

The Weber findings raised some questions. Did the inner-city schools with a more traditional focus do better because the reading tests they used emphasized the schools' traditional approaches? Would they have done as well if the children had taken reading tests that focused on the outcomes favored by progressive, student-centered schools?

For reading in the earliest grades all reading measures are heavily weighted to measure skills, because skills are the most essential components. Further, student-centered reading tests were not widely available in the early 1970s, but the reading research literature has found for nearly 100 years that the different tests are highly correlated (Weber, 1971).

It should be noted that most of the early studies on the effectiveness of the different methods were done in the early grades, when the low-income children had not yet acquired sufficient background in vocabulary and reading skills. Without these skills, such students need teacher-directed methods to help them to "catch up." Once they have acquired the basic skills, these children might benefit from a more student-centered focus as much as children do who are from middle-class backgrounds.

Two additional studies of the reading of low-income children have recently come to my attention. Mann and Lawrence (1980–1981) reviewed seven research studies on school effectiveness and found great consistency in their findings. In fact, their findings are quite similar to those already presented here. Effective schools for the poor have traditional features that Mann and Lawrence (1980–1981, p. 7) enumerate as:

1. *Principal's characteristics,* especially strong leadership.
2. *Teacher's characteristics,* especially high expectations.
3. *School "climate" or atmosphere,* especially one that is conducive to learning.
4. *Instructional emphasis* that is concentrated on pupil acquisition of basic skills.
5. *Pupil evaluation* that is frequent and linked to what children and teachers do next.

A later review by Samuels (1988) found essentially the same characteristics effective with children of low socioeconomic status as were found in the foregoing reviews and studies:

The most recent studies of effective schools indicate there are some subtle differences between upper and lower socioeconomic schools. . . . In low socioeconomic schools, the emphasis is on basic skills, homework expectations are moderate, instructional leaders exert high levels of control over instruction, home–school links tend to be moderate to weak, and rewards given to students are extrinsic and frequent. In high socioeconomic schools, curricular emphasis extends beyond basic skills, homework expectations are high, instructional leaders exert moderate control over instruction, home–school links are strong, and rewards are more intrinsic and less frequent. (Samuels, 1988, p. 8)

In England, at about the same time, Rutter, Maughan, Mortimer, and Ouston (1979) compared the behavior, achievement on standardized tests, and employment success of low-income students at twelve high schools with different educational aims. They noted that some were "firmly committed to the development of children's personalities," others to "the passing of examinations as the first requirement" (p. 41).

Those schools that emphasized academic matters—as demonstrated by the prevalence of homework, teacher expectations of student performance, the display of students' work on school walls, teaching time, and several other factors—made better progress.

The findings as a whole . . . suggest that children tended to make better progress both behaviourally and academically, in schools which placed an appropriate emphasis on academic matters. This emphasis might be reflected in a well planned curriculum, in the kinds of expectations teachers had of the children they taught, and in the setting and marking of homework. (Rutter et al., 1979)

Teachers in the more successful schools also spent higher proportions of their time interacting with the class as a whole rather than with individual pupils.

SCHOOLS AND LOW-INCOME CHILDREN

Research studies, experience, and the early writings on education all agree that children of the rich do better in academic learning in all schools than children of the poor (Eppenstein, 1966). But the magnitude of the difference was brought home strongly and dramatically by the now classic study of school achievement by James Coleman and his associates (1966). They found that the socioeconomic status of the child's parents and their educational attainment had the strongest influence on the child's school learning—stronger even than the amount of funding for the school, for example. Indeed, this conclusion soon led to the popular interpretation that what schools taught mattered little in school achievement. What mattered most was the background of the parents, these findings seemed to suggest.

Yet, if one looks at the fine print of the Coleman report, one can find substantial evidence that how students were taught in school and the quality of the teachers who taught them *did* make a considerable difference. Generally, the more verbal the teacher (i.e., the higher the score on a test of word meanings) and the more professional the teacher (e.g., whether the teacher belonged to professional associations), the better the achievement of his or her students. Coleman found further that good teaching, while important for all students, was especially beneficial for low-achieving, low-income students.

More recently the National Assessment of Educational Progress (Mullis et al., 1993) reported that the children of the rich scored considerably higher on all national tests than the children of the poor. This disparity in performance was observable in reading, writing, mathematics, science, and social studies tests given in the 1970s through the 1990s. The international comparison of reading achievement in fifteen countries by Robert L. Thorndike (1973) found that higher reading achievement was positively associated with higher socioeconomic status, both within countries and across borders.

These research studies and surveys led to various projects designed to raise the achievement of low-income children. Among them was the Effective Schools Program directed by Ron Edmonds of Harvard University during the 1980s. He proposed to raise the achievement of poor children by focusing on the following: strong leadership by the principal, a healthy school climate, high expectations of achievement, a basic skills emphasis, and frequent assessment. Note that these characteristics are very similar to the key features identified by Mann and Lawrence (1980–1981), as well as Weber (1971) and Rutter et al. (1979), and that they are primarily traditional, teacher-centered concerns.

Overall, the Effective Schools Program focused on instruction. Teachers were expected to spend more time on instruction than on other activities. There was also more monitoring of instruction by the principal. Teachers were expected to be more task oriented, to give more homework, and to set high expectations for students. Achievement was the first goal of the school, and it was believed that more could be achieved when the whole class or large groups were taught together instead of trying to gear instruction to the needs of individuals. Direct instruction was preferred to indirect instruction. Teachers expected to be observed and evaluated. Again, most of these were traditional-type approaches.

The Effective Schools Program (Edmonds, 1979) viewed the education of the 1970s as providing too little instruction and too little homework, as too play-oriented rather than achievement-oriented, and as favoring too much individualization that often resulted in needless confusion. Similar to Delpit, Edmonds preferred a traditional, teacher-centered education for low-income children.

The Effective Schools movement did not last very long. It seemed to fade away, and yet, recent studies of socioeconomic effects on achievement point to the importance of programs that provide academic support, especially for students from disadvantaged backgrounds.

OPEN EDUCATION IN AN INNER CITY: A CASE STUDY

In his book *Open Education and the American School* (1972), Roland Barth gives us a moving firsthand account of an experiment with open education in an inner-city school. What is striking about the open education experiment is that, in spite of the high hopes and hard work of the participating teachers and administrators, it failed.

It was carried out in a middle-sized community with a mixed population. The average class size was twenty-three. The problems of the school and children, according to Barth, were "the problems of urban education and of so-called 'deprived' children everywhere: difficulty in reading, writing, and speaking the English language; poor conceptual ability; limited capacity for social interaction; and negative self concept" (Barth, 1972, p. 114).

The teachers who participated in the experiment had a prefer-ence for student-centered education:

> [They] believed that education is experience encountered, not knowledge transmitted, and that an experience curriculum is as appropriate (or more appropriate) for low-economic-status chil-dren as for high-economic-status children, for blacks as for whites. (p. 137)

The great disappointment for the teachers was that their views on open education did not fit well with the expectations of the children and their parents. Open education did not seem to work with these children. They expressed neither joy in response to the experience curriculum nor appreciation for the freedom and open-ness to learn that had been anticipated. Their parents were even more displeased with open education. They wanted their children to learn from the teachers and from books, not from arts and crafts.

Worth noting is that the dissatisfactions these parents expressed closely paralleled those of immigrant parents in New York City in the 1920s and those of the parents of students in the Gary, Indiana, schools who objected to progressive education for their children.

I will present Barth's findings in some detail since they are consistent with the accumulated research and with observations on how best to teach low-income status children found in the litera-ture for at least a century.

RESPONSES OF THE CHILDREN TO THE OPEN EDUCATION EXPERIMENT

Open education, like other student-centered approaches, assumes that children learn by exploring, making choices, and by setting and solving their own problems,

> Following theory and intuition, they [the teachers] encouraged children to make decisions. But many children had limited ca-pacity to attend to a task; the more options made available to them, the more difficult that attending became. A rich environ-ment of manipulative materials only made it less likely that a child could focus on any one. (Barth, 1972, pp. 138–139)

The teachers had difficulty keeping order in the classroom. With no restrictions from the teachers, the children often hung around outside the bathrooms and at the water fountains. They even left the classrooms when the teacher's back was turned.

Controlling the children was difficult. Barth noted that the children seemed to want "stability and evidence of concern in a familiar form. The open classrooms and their teachers provided neither" (p. 139).

There were difficulties with discipline. A fourth-grade teacher, while teaching math, told her class that the teacher in the adjoining classroom had complained about the noise they were making. She asked, "How are we going to keep the noise down?" Their responses were revealing:

> Tape our mouths shut.
> Kick the noisy ones out of class.
> Punish us.
> Let's go somewhere else for math.
> Send a note home to the bad people's parents.
> They make noise and bother us; why can't we make noise?
> (pp. 139–140)

Barth comments on these remedies:

> What characterizes this imaginative collection of remedies is that each depends on the teacher to control the children's behavior. No one suggested that the class control itself; no one said, "We will have to try to whisper, not shout." (p. 140)

Barth also comments on the disappointment of the open education teachers. They attempted to become "more traditional," but they found it difficult to do so. When they tried to adopt more traditional practices, they could not. They had not been prepared for the traditional role that was expected and being demanded of them. They were unable to take on the role of managing the children and transmitting knowledge to them. Adopting some traditional practices like requiring a "lav pass" did not solve the problem. One teacher observed, "What I need is a cram course in being a traditional teacher" (p. 143).

The open educators in the experiment were stunned to find

that the children rejected their open, facilitating approach to learning as much, if not more, than the traditional practices. Barth notes that this occurs often in the United States, where many beginning teachers are drawn to open education. "Many have turned to open education through insecurity; they are permissive because they are afraid that if they are strong, the children will reject them" (p. 144).

RESISTANCE FROM PARENTS

The parents in the open education schools did not favor the open education (student-centered) approach. They preferred a traditional pattern where teachers teach and students learn. Parents who visited the open classrooms

> were astonished and angered by what they saw: children with their backs to the teacher, playing with animals, games, and each other; teachers called by their first names; children eating candy or potato chips; children swearing at other children; spitballs being openly exchanged. The parents considered such behavior disrespectful and a source of intense embarrassment. (pp. 147–148)

Parents also questioned the lack of a curriculum. " 'Where are the 3R's? All I see is crafts, weaving, making things out of wood, leather, yarn; weighing things. Where are the *books*?' " (p. 149).

Parents also asked about homework and about discipline—the common signs to them of an education. They also asked for more phonics and drill homework. They complained about the high grades given by teachers. " 'She has been too free with marks on report cards. My child got all A's and B's, and I *know* my child is no A or B student' " (p. 153). Other grievances were that the children weren't learning and weren't being taught to behave, and that good students were falling behind because the others took attention away from them. One parent complained that one child was swearing at the teacher and the teacher didn't do anything about it.

The greatest concern of the parents was that open education might hinder their child's advancement toward a productive life. Sounding very much like today's CEOs of American industry, who are strong boosters of education, they pleaded for a good elementary education for their child in order to meet the later challenges for success in school and in work. " 'We want our children to go to high school, to college, to get a good white-collar job, to have a home, a car, and raise a family. In short, we want them to do what *you* (whites) have done' " (p. 156).

Many of the parents reminded the teachers and administrators that they had had an educational experience in which they acquired knowledge and skills. They learned to be respectful and obedient. This is what they wanted for their children.

> "If our children have the same kind of educational experience, *they too* will make it. . . . But, since our children are starting with many strikes against them, since many are already behind in reading, writing, and arithmetic, and self-control, they will have to have your educational experience, only *more so*. More respect, more obedience, more authority, more homework, more books, more discipline." (p. 156)

SOCIAL CLASS DIFFERENCES
AND EDUCATIONAL APPROACHES

The research findings, as well as the experiences of teachers and the preferences of parents just reported, point to the benefits of a teacher-centered educational approach for low-income children. The key factor seems to be the lower-socioeconomic-status child's lack of school-related experiences when he or she enters school. This would explain why, generally, lower-socioeconomic-status children do better in more structured, direct-teaching classes than they do in student-centered classrooms. Rosenshine (1987), for example, found that children in the primary grades, and particularly low-income children, did better when they had direct rather than indirect instruction. Similarly, Gage (1978; Gage & Berliner, 1992) and other investigators found fewer differences between higher- than lower-socioeconomic-status children when they received direct instruction.

This phenomenon is also found in learning math, writing, and science. The underlying factor seems to be what the children know and what they do not know when they enter school. If what is being taught is at least partially known by the student, either a teacher-centered or student-centered approach seems to work. But, if what is taught is relatively unknown, direct instruction works better whether the students come from low-income or middle-class families.

The search for the best teaching methods for students with different levels of knowledge, skill, and background has a long history in education. It was the guiding principle behind Maria Montessori's direct methods, which were originally designed for children with limited abilities. Later Montessori found them beneficial for poor children. In recent years Montessori methods have been used even more frequently with the children of the rich (Chall, 1967).

Several years ago teachers in Houston who worked with large numbers of low-income children requested that they be permitted to return to a highly structured reading program instead of the open, whole-language, student-centered approach that had been adopted by their school district in the late 1980s. They claimed that the reading scores of low-income children had declined since the more open, whole language method was used. More recently, California, one of the first states to use a whole-language approach, returned to a more traditional reading program when its students' reading test scores, particularly among low-income children, fell almost to the bottom of U.S. state rankings.

Indeed, the evidence on the superiority of structured, teacher-centered methods for low-socioeconomic-status children is so consistent over the years that it would be difficult to reject it. The words of low-income parents expressing their dissatisfaction with progressive, student-centered education are much the same today, or in 1980, as they were in 1920. Low-income parents in the 1920s and still today want their children to learn reading, writing, arithmetic, and to succeed in the real world. They do not want student-centered education, because it is not as helpful in teaching the basic skills and it does not provide the discipline that children need.

Other socioeconomic groups also seem to have preferences of their own for their children. Those in the middle class seem to have been the early enthusiasts of experimental, progressive schools that promised individualization of instruction and a concern for the total child—not for academic achievement alone, but for social and emotional development as well. After all, if their children were having difficulties with their academic learning, the parents had the means to hire private tutors.

The preference among the upper class, however, seems to be for a traditional, classic education (see Powell, 1996). Ironically, the rich and poor alike apparently prefer the same kind of education for their children—a classic, teacher-centered education—while it is the middle class that seems to prefer the progressive, student-centered approaches.

What lies behind these preferences? Low-socioeconomic-status parents realize more than anyone that, if their children are to have any chance of "making it" in life, they will first have to "make it" in school, and they know that it all starts with reading, writing, and arithmetic.

For upper-class parents, the choice of a traditional school probably stems from their future plans for their children—for them to enter prestigious colleges and traditional professions. But, even if their children do not ultimately pursue those traditional professions, parents see a traditional education as good preparation for other high-level positions.

Progressive, open schools seem more congenial to the middle-class, whose children come to school with knowledge and skills acquired at home and in nursery school, from being read to, from educational toys, and more recently from computers. But, even with this rich educational stimulation provided before the age of six, many middle-class parents have, for nearly a decade, kept their children at home for an additional year, from ages six to seven, to give them a more secure start in first grade. Thus, in spite of the educational advantages of middle-class children, some middle-class parents do not feel quite confident enough to have their child "compete" in a progressive, student-centered first grade.

The difference in the educational preferences of middle- and low-income parents is found also in how they help their children learn. In a book for parents on how to prepare their preschool child for literacy (McLane & McNamee, 1990; see Chall, 1991, for a review of the McLane & McNamee book), an emphasis is placed on divergent thinking and creativity, that is, having the child learn mainly through discovery. Although the authors do not state it directly, it is quite clear that their teaching suggestions are offered mainly for middle-class, highly educated parents.

By way of contrast, McLane and McNamee present also a description of how a working class mother taught her child to read. She first taught him the alphabet from a book bought at Woolworth's. After he learned the letters, she read aloud with him from the Bible. This is, essentially, a traditional, teacher-centered approach.

Many low-income parents provide a traditional education for their children by sending them to Catholic school, even though they are not themselves Catholic. What they seek for their children, they say, is discipline and an emphasis on learning. These low-income parents believe that the parochial schools teach the basic skills better than the public schools (see Coleman et al., 1966; Bryk et al., 1993).

STUDENTS WITH LEARNING DISABILITIES

Traditional, teacher-centered approaches have also been preferred in educating those with difficulty in learning—those who have learning disabilities irrespective of social class. This was noted as early as the 1930s by Samuel T. Orton (1937) and others (e.g., Harris, 1940). Indeed, it is the approach that has been used in most remedial reading programs from the 1920s to the present (Chall & Peterson, 1986).

The traditional, teacher-centered education works for children with learning difficulties because it provides more structure and more direct instruction than does a progressive, student-centered approach. Even during the great popularity of progressive education, remedial instruction continued to have a traditional, teacher-centered emphasis. When direct teaching of phonics was abandoned by most teachers of reading in the 1920s and 1930s, in compliance with progressive education, successful remedial reading programs continued to teach phonics (Chall, 1967; Monroe, 1932; Orton, 1937). And even in the 1990s the strongest feature of Reading Recovery—a new approach to remedial reading that described itself originally as a progressive approach—is its structure. Successful remedial programs in math have similar characteristics, namely, direct instruction and structure.

SUMMARY

A review of research on social class differences and educational approaches suggests that a traditional, teacher-centered approach results in better achievement among poor children and among those with learning difficulties at all social levels. Significantly, it is also the approach preferred for privileged children who attend prestigious private schools.

The qualitative research indicates that low-socioeconomic-status parents have tended to question the value of progressive, student-centered education for their children. In the 1920s and 1930s, particularly, poor New York City immigrant parents rebelled when they learned that their children were to be taught using student-centered curricula and methods. They still do not favor it today.

Middle-class parents who have children with reading and other learning difficulties have also tended to be critical of progressive, student-centered education. But they find ways to foster their children's achievement, mainly by hiring private tutors or sending them to special tutoring schools that use traditional approaches.

One of the factors in a preference for either a teacher-centered or a student-centered approach is the importance of basic skills in a child's educational development. Difficulty in learning the basics of reading, writing, or mathematics can be a problem for the rich as well as the poor child, and for the intellectually able or challenged alike. But it is particularly handicapping for poor children. If rich children require more instruction in basic skills, their parents can get it for them, an option not open to low-income parents whose children may therefore fall further and further behind in achievement. By the twelfth grade they average four years below their expected grade level in reading (NAEP, 1971).

CHAPTER 9

—

Parents, the Media,
and Other
Nonschool Educators

On the *McNeil–Lehrer News Hour* (February 1993), Jim Lehrer asked a childhood friend of Henry Cisneros to what he attributed Cisneros's success. What made it possible for him to become U.S. Secretary of Housing and Urban Development from his modest beginnings as a poor Hispanic boy? Without hesitation, the friend said it had been Cisneros's mother. When his friends went out to play ball, Cisneros's mother made him stay home and read *Ivanhoe*. He went to a Catholic elementary school and to the most demanding Catholic high school in San Antonio, then to Texas A&M, and then got a White House Fellowship. Later he got a master's degree and doctorate in urban affairs from Harvard.

Spike Lee, the African American movie producer, director, and writer, spoke of similar family influences. In a television interview several years ago, he noted that his mother took him regularly to see plays when he was a small boy and made him sit up and stay awake. She also exposed him to classical music when he was quite young.

Richard Rodriguez, a writer and television commentator, wrote in his autobiography, *The Hunger of Memory* (1982), that his parents, immigrants from Mexico, took great pride in his school achievement. He was also encouraged by his remedial reading teacher, a kind, elderly nun, who introduced him to the reading of classics.

The public library made it possible for children of immigrant parents to become readers at an early age. Irving Kristol, former managing editor of *Commentary*, wrote that his father was too tired to read to him. He did not have books of his own, but he borrowed them from the public library and became an avid reader (1995).

In an earlier generation small family businesses no doubt contributed to the school achievement of children whose parents were themselves barely literate in English. Helping out in the store developed the child's language and math skills. Some of our most eminent scientists grew up in the living area above a candy or a grocery store. Their "helping out" no doubt contributed to their learning of mathematics and reading, and also to their problem-solving ability.

Jesse Jackson, at a Washington, DC, conference on literacy in 1978, took a strong position on parents' responsibility for their children's school achievement. There is a need, he said, for students to spend as much time on academics as on sports. In his view, parents should be required to sign a pledge that they will monitor two hours of homework daily, go to school to pick up their child's report card, and go to the board of education to pick up the child's test scores once a year.

Some parents have different views of their role in the education of their children. I recall that when high school students in a Massachusetts suburb complained that the required summer reading list prepared by their teachers—which included such titles as *A Tale of Two Cities*, *The Glass Menagerie*, *Jane Eyre*, and *The Adventures of Tom Sawyer*—was too boring, too long, and too hard, their parents agreed. They said they had never heard of half the books. The school board then changed the requirement. The books were to be listed, but the students could select for reading only those they wanted to read.

Even a child's achievement in first grade reading depends a

great deal on what the parent does. In some highly respected, affluent, suburban schools, some parents engage private reading tutors for their children even before they enter first grade. This is done because it is generally known that the schools are not successful in teaching reading. Parents keep their child in that school because of other benefits—the school atmosphere is a happy one, there is respect for the individual child, and it is strong in art and science.

Homework is increasing in many schools, even in the first grade (Winerip, 1999, p. 6). Many parents resent it. Homework, they say, takes leisure time away from the child. And the parents resent the time they are expected to give to their child's homework. They think teachers are putting an added burden on them.

The vignettes I have just recounted illustrate that parents, as well as schools and teachers, tend to prefer either a traditional, teacher-centered or a progressive, student-centered approach to their child's education. The mothers of Henry Cisneros and Spike Lee took a traditional position. They introduced their sons to classic literature and art, setting standards that resemble those usually found in private schools. They did not leave the child's leisure time to his or her expressed interests, as is done in student-centered programs.

Jesse Jackson's advice to parents also has a traditional ring. In essence he said that parents should supervise homework and pay attention to the child's test scores and report cards—as traditional, teacher-centered educators have long maintained down through the years. He knew students were more interested in sports than in their studies, but he said they need to spend more time on studies.

Several of the other vignettes reveal preferences that are more student-centered—parents want to cooperate with the school, but they resent the time it takes. Others support their child's preference for a voluntary reading list instead of the schools' more rigorous required list.

What are the effects of these different views and actions of parents on the school achievement of their children? There is a rather large literature (and it seems to be growing) that parents have a considerable influence on the child's academic achievement. Before discussing these studies, I present a brief historical overview of the changes in practices and attitudes on the role of families in a child's education.

In U.S. schools prior to the 1900s, parents were held responsible for assuring their children's school attendance, buying their books, and seeing that they did what the teachers required. With the shift to student-centered education in the 1920s, the role of parents became less clear. This can be seen in the changes in student report cards. From an emphasis on exact reporting of academic achievement (letter grades or percentages for each subject), report cards began to use descriptive terms instead. Some schools even stopped sending report cards home and used teacher–parent conferences instead.

Parents were encouraged to be more relaxed about the child's academic learning. This can be seen in parents' attitudes toward early reading. In her first study of early reading (1966), Dolores Durkin found that few children of middle-class educated parents were early readers. Durkin's interviews revealed that the better-educated parents did not teach their children to read at home because at that time it was not considered good practice by teachers and reading specialists in modern schools.* Therefore they did not encourage their children's early reading. The less-educated mothers did not know that it was not considered good practice to teach their preschool children to read, and they taught them to.

In a follow-up study years later (1974–1975), Durkin found a larger number of early readers in educated, middle-class families. Why the change? By then, there had been a change in the views of modern educators and child development experts toward early reading. It was no longer considered harmful to teach preschoolers to read. It was, by then, considered helpful to the children's education.

Parents' attitudes toward achievement are greatly influenced by teachers and child psychologists. The more educated the parents, it would seem, the more they are influenced by the preferences of the school and the child experts. The influence, of course, is also from home to school. And the changes in society affect both. One cannot overlook the influence of Dr. Benjamin Spock on children's

---

*See in this connection Harper Lee's *To Kill a Mockingbird*, where Scout was told by her teacher to tell her father to stop teaching her to read.

education in school and in the home. Spock advised millions of parents to ease up on their control of their children—to use less authoritarian ways. He said, in essence, "Trust yourself. Don't be afraid to do what you think." Dewey and his followers were having similar influences on children in school.

It is difficult, therefore, to be precise about the greater effects of homes and schools on student achievement. Both are important in a child's education. Even factors that can clearly be attributed to the home, on further examination, can be seen as being influenced also by the school. Thus Steinberg (1996) found that too many hours spent in after-school jobs were associated with lower grades among teenagers. Is this a home factor or a school factor? Of course, parents who approve of their own teenager's long hours of work must be held responsible. But is the school free of responsibility? Couldn't the school set standards for academic work that would make long hours of work on an after-school job impossible? But Steinberg notes that, instead of counseling these students to cut down on their work hours, schools often adjust to the students' job schedules by accepting less demanding school work from them. This is quite different from the way prestigious private schools plan the schoolwork schedule of their students, which is more demanding and consistent for all students (see Powell, 1996).

THE RESEARCH EVIDENCE

The earliest research findings on home influences—whether based on observation or on quantitative research—were that the socioeconomic status of the child's family had a strong influence on how well he or she learned in school. This was observed by educators hundreds of years ago. In recent times it was brought out dramatically in the 1966 research of Coleman and his associates. As noted earlier, their extensive analyses of student achievement found that the children of parents who were more highly educated and economically more stable did better in school than those of lesser-endowed parents. Indeed, they concluded that these family differences had a stronger influence on student achievement than the funds expended by the schools the students attended.

Another nonschool factor found to be highly related to academic achievement is ethnic background. Steinberg (1996) concluded from his recent analysis of achievement among 20,000 teenagers in nine high schools, hundreds of their parents, and dozens of their teachers that ethnic differences have an even greater influence on school achievement than socioeconomic status and school characteristics.

In spite of the substantial correlations between social status and school achievement, many have argued that the value of knowing this relationship is limited for educational policy and practice. Further, explaining achievement by social class and ethnicity may be damaging to children if teachers set their expectations by them, then proceeding to treat the children in accordance with those expectations (Kellaghan, Sloane, Alvarez, & Bloom, 1993, p. 42).

Because of the limitations of family status factors, many researchers began to look at home process variables—behaviors and conditions in the home, irrespective of social status, that are related to school achievement. Some of these are related to socioeconomic status, but they need not be. They include such factors as parents' expectations for the child's success in school, availability in the home of books and other reading materials, and the amount of attention the family gives to the child's schoolwork (Chall, Jacobs, & Baldwin, 1990).

The home process variables that have been found to be the best predictors of school learning were classified as follows by Kellaghan et al. (1993, p. 136):

1. *Work habits of the family:* The degree of routine in the management of the home, the emphasis on regularity in the use of space and time, and the priority given to schoolwork over other pleasurable activities.
2. *Academic guidance and support:* The availability and quality of the help and encouragement that parents give their children in their schoolwork and the conditions they provide to support schoolwork.
3. *Stimulation to explore and discuss ideas and events:* Opportunities provided by the home to explore ideas, events, and the larger environment.

4. *Language environment:* Opportunities in the home for the development of the correct and effective use of language.

5. *Academic aspirations and expectations:* Parents' aspirations for their children, the standards they set for children's school achievement, and their interest in and knowledge of children's school experiences.

It is interesting to note that these home process variables are similar to the school factors that have been reported to have a strong influence on student achievement. Thus, the processes and characteristics that enhance academic achievement are essentially the same—whether found in the home or in the school. For example, such characteristics as order and routine, high expectations of achievement, language and intellectual stimulation, when found in the home, enhance school achievement as they do when found in the school (see Bryk et al., 1993; Chall, 1987; Chall & Feldmann, 1966; Powell, 1996).

Kellaghan et al. make a similar point stating that: When home and school have divergent approaches to life and learning, children are likely to suffer in their school learning. Conversely, when home and school have similar emphasis on motivation and learning, children are likely to do well. Socioeconomic level or cultural background, on the other hand,

> need not determine how well a child does at school. Parents from a variety of cultural backgrounds and with different levels of education, income, or occupational status can and do provide stimulating home environments that support and encourage the learning of their children. It is what parents do in the home rather than their status that is important. (Kellaghan et al., 1993, p. 145)

Overall, "the process variables in the home predict scholastic ability and achievement better than do measures of social class, family structure, or parental characteristics" (Kellaghan, 1993, p. 55). However, home processes "are not unrelated to the home's socioeconomic status. Homes that are classified as high in social status are likely to be treated higher on home process variables than are homes classified as low in social status" (p. 55).

What is remarkable about the home process variables is that they are related to school achievement in different socioeconomic groups, in urban as well as in rural environments in the United States, in other Western countries, and in developing countries (Kellaghan et al., 1993, p. 56).

When home process factors are turned into home intervention programs for parents, the results have been very good. "Numerous comprehensive reviews of the results of such programs over the years indicate that efforts to help parents become stronger partners in their children's learning can have a significant positive impact on children's cognitive development, school performance, and social functioning" (Kellaghan et al., 1993, p. 119).

The students in the Steinberg study reported little personal involvement with their studies, not because they found their studies too difficult, but because, on the contrary, they found them insufficiently demanding. They also lost interest because of "the absence of any consequences for failing to meet even these minimal demands" (Steinberg, 1996, p. 68).

Very little homework was assigned in the high schools they attended—"the majority of high school students spend four or fewer hours per week on homework. Only one in six spends ten or more hours each week—that is, the equivalent of two hours on each school day—studying outside of school" (Steinberg, 1996, p. 68). What, then, do students do with their time? Most of it is spent "hanging around" with friends. The next most popular activity is working at a part-time job. International comparisons show that high school students in other countries spend much more time on homework—up to five times as much for some countries—and considerably less time hanging out with friends and doing part-time work.

Steinberg comments on this: "If we really want to understand why our students fare so much worse on tests of achievement than their foreign counterparts, perhaps we should be looking less at differences in our countries' schools, and more at differences in our teenager's lives" (1996, p. 68). Very little of the typical U.S. high school student's time—between fifteen and twenty hours per week, or about 15 percent of their waking hours—is spent on tasks related to learning and achievement. Compared to others in the industrialized world, our students have the fewest demands put on them in terms of school-related activities.

Steinberg's focus on the home as an explanation for the low academic achievement of adolescents does not overlook the responsibility of the school. Indeed, a vicious circle exists between schools and homes:

> Thus, while it is true that very little homework is assigned in American schools, this is partly because students often do not do what their teachers ask of them: more than a third of the students we surveyed say they do not do the homework they are given. (Steinberg, 1996, p. 69)

In his concluding remarks, Steinberg comes down stronger on the side of it being the school's responsibility for academic decline. He notes that the less schools demand, the more students spend their time earning pocket money and socializing with friends. The more they work at part-time jobs, the less interested they become in school. As students become increasingly disengaged, schools tend to demand less, have lower standards, and need to search more for ways to keep students interested.

Another of Steinberg's findings is that high school students do not associate doing well in school with later success at work. They recognize that having a high school diploma is better than being a dropout and that a college degree is better than a high school diploma. According to Steinberg, they do not associate later success with doing well in school or in what they learn in school. What seems to matter is whether they graduate.

Similar to other studies (see Powell, 1996; Bryk, Lee, & Holland, 1993; Coleman et al., 1996; Weber, 1971) Steinberg found that where the expectations and demands of the school are high, where students work harder, the social and cultural factors of the home appear to have a smaller influence.

Also of interest in Steinberg's findings is the declining achievement of immigrant students; that is, the longer they are in the United States, the lower their academic progress. Those students who have been living here longer are less committed to doing well in school. Generally, more recent immigrants spend more time on homework, are more oriented to doing well in school, and are more likely to have friends who think academic achievement is important. They are also more likely to attribute their school success and failure to effort and hard work and downplay the significance of luck, native ability, and other factors that are out of one's control (Steinberg, 1996, pp. 97–98).

A more optimistic view of adolescents' attitudes toward learning was reported recently by Diane Ravitch (1998). She discussed a study by the Public Agenda Foundation, based on polling and focus groups, in which it was concluded that American teenagers want higher academic and behavioral standards in their schools.

Most youngsters—of all social and ethnic backgrounds—agreed that schools seem to expect little of them. Therefore they do just enough to meet minimal standards. The great majority said if they tried harder they could do better.

African American students, particularly, complained about a lack of emphasis on "basic skills" and about poor teaching. They disliked it that students get promoted who don't deserve it.

Students in private schools were more positive about their schools than students in public schools. They were "far less likely to complain about the absence of challenge" (Ravitch, 1998, p. 77). American teenagers, Ravitch reports, "hunger for structure, discipline and more rigorous standards" (p. 77).

RECENT TRENDS IN THE ROLE OF PARENTS

There appears to be a growing emphasis on the home in student achievement. Indeed, it would seem appropriate that, if the schools' demands on students' academic time and accomplishments continue to decrease, more *should be* expected from parents.

This lesson was illustrated in a recent *Good Morning America* show in which a young working mother of a sixth grader advised other parents to keep their children constructively occupied while they are home alone. "Give your child a little assignment to do—like reading a book and writing an essay on what he or she thinks of it." The TV host thought this was very original. Was it possible that he did not know that this was a rather routine homework assignment prior to the popularity of student-centered learning? No one seemed to notice the reversal of roles played by the school and the home.

There are now a variety of commercially produced school-type videos and computer programs for preschoolers and children in the elementary grades. These programs, made for home use, contain school-like activities and emphasize fun while promising to teach reading, math, and other school subjects.

There is also an increasing variety of home programs designed to teach phonics to young children, illiterate adults, and children with reading problems. The commercial success of such programs as *Hooked on Phonics* reflects the growing trend for parents to participate in, and even take over, the child's academic learning. The existence of these commercial programs for home use may also be a sign of the school's slackening off on the teaching of basic skills. Thus, as the schools ease up on the teaching of phonics, parents take it over, buying self-teaching commercial programs or hiring private tutors to do it. This was, in fact, what a parent, who was a professional educator, said he did. Although he was pleased with the value of the whole-language program in his children's school, he said he hired a tutor privately to teach them phonics just to make sure that they had the best instruction.

It would appear that parents of young children are increasingly "rushing in" where they have doubts about the school's meeting their child's needs. They may do it together with other parents in some kind of "political action." Or they may do it more privately, such as hiring a tutor "on the side" or sending the child for special help to a tutoring school—a solution possible for the affluent but not for those of limited means. Thus, we have another possible reason why achievement is positively correlated with parents' income, and why the weaker the school program, the greater the difference in achievement of children of the rich and children of the poor.

School programs that depend on greater parent involvement may also have some unanticipated consequences. It is unrealistic to expect parents who work full time, who are single parents, and particularly those who have a limited education to help their children with their studies. They can, of course, encourage their children and support their efforts. But it seems the involvement that some schools expect of parents is more than most are willing or able to manage.

TV, COMPUTERS, AND OTHER TECHNOLOGY

There is general agreement that TV has some effect on the attitudes, values, and behaviors of children. There is less consensus on the effects of TV on school achievement, although there is general agreement that the more time spent watching TV, the less time left for reading and other school-related activities. Indeed, the National Assessment of Educational Progress has found that, among fourth graders, the greater the amount of TV watching, the lower the reading scores (NAEP, 1996).

Several years ago I undertook a study with my graduate students that sought to explain this difference that I had observed, that TV had a positive effect on the vocabulary of younger children and a negative effect on older students. We thought the answers might be found in the complexity of the language heard on TV in relation to the complexity of the child's language. We analyzed the language in widely viewed TV shows and compared it to the language used by the children and found that most TV programs used a very simple language—some as low as a second- or third-grade level. Radio programs that were popular with children at earlier periods used much more complex language. *The Lone Ranger*, for example, used language on a seventh- to eighth-grade level.

We proposed that, since the TV shows watched by preschoolers and first graders contained some words that were not already known to them, their vocabularies grew by watching these programs. But the students in the middle grades who already knew most of the words did not gain in vocabulary knowledge.

The essential factor in learning language from TV is the level of difficulty of the TV language in relation to the language the viewer has already acquired. The viewer will learn language from TV if its complexity is above the level he or she can already understand and use. Popular radio shows used more challenging language than most of the TV shows watched by children. And books, of course, can present the greatest challenge for acquiring language.

COMPUTERS

Computers are considered such an important tool for learning that the lack of computers is often given as a reason for the low achievement of students who do not have access to them. This is claimed even though the evidence for the educational value of computers is still far from complete. Yet, there is a growing confidence in the educational value of computers in the home as well as in the school.

Several kinds of computer uses are available both for the school and the home—the computer as a tutor or textbook, the computer as a research tool, and the computer as an instrument for enhancing creativity and problem-solving ability.*

Probably the greatest home use of computers is as a tutor, teacher, or textbook—for teaching reading, phonics, math, spelling, vocabulary—designed to bring the users to a higher level of knowledge and skill. There are tutor programs designed for preschoolers up to college students.

Entire encyclopedias, almanacs, thesauri, atlases, and other reference materials are now available for computer use, when formerly they were available only in books. As with such references in book form, a great deal of responsibility is placed on the user to know what knowledge is needed and how to use it. As with books, the user also needs to have the language and reading skills to match the language used on the computer.

A third form of computer use, for developing creativity and problem-solving ability, has been favored by Seymour Papert of the Massachusetts Institute of Technology. In his book *The Connected Family* (1996), Papert writes that computers can be most effective in providing an opportunity for the child to explore the world independently. This use is particularly appropriate today, he says, because children are becoming more independent earlier. The independent use of computers, where students are not provided with the questions and answers, is said to encourage independent thinking and problem solving. According to Papert, free exploration with a computer makes possible the continuation of the "learning instinct" that is often stopped by the school, and acts as a building block to create freely.

HOME SCHOOLING

In 1995 it was estimated that about 600,000 children in the United States were being educated at home. By 1998, the estimate was closer to 1 million.

Home schooling started among parents who were not content

*I wish to thank Emily Marston for these categories.

with what the public schools were offering. They sought a more structured, traditional type of education for their children, that is, greater emphasis on knowledge and skills. Many also wanted religious training, which the public schools did not provide.

On a public radio talk show hosted by Christopher Lyden (November 27, 1996, "The Connection," WBUR, Boston) the parents who were most vocal about home schooling seemed to be seeking a more open, progressive education for their children. They chose home schooling because they wanted their children to appreciate learning—not to wait to be told when to learn and what to learn. One mother who preferred a student-centered education said she did not want her child to be hand-fed. If she is interested in dinosaurs, she should be permitted to study dinosaurs for a year. Further, children do not need to be taught. They learn and parents learn. All they need is books, libraries, and the community.

A mother contrasted home schooling with regular schooling as follows: the home schoolers talk of loving history, for example; the children in regular school say that they are good at history. Thus, home schoolers study for the love of the subject, while regular schools stress achievement.

Another mother said that she was dissatisfied with both public and private schools because they do not let the parents know what the children are learning, and they give little attention to each child's learning.

In response to the widespread concern that parents do not have the certification or experience to teach, many said that all that is needed is to be committed. Parents can find out what they need to know as they go along. They can call on different mentors; scientists and artists in the community can be asked to give their expertise.

Lyden asked whether children who do well in home school are of above-average ability. Could ordinary children do well in home schooling? The response was that those children who are not doing well in school do better in home school.

It is of interest to note that no one referred to any existing research evidence on the effects of home schooling. It would, of course, be important to know whether home schooling works only with certain kinds of children and certain kinds of parents—also, how it affects social development and the ability to get along with many kinds of children, an objective of public schools.*

NONSCHOOL INFLUENCES ON ACHIEVEMENT: THE ROLE OF PARENTS

The role that parents are asked to play in the education of their young child's education seems to be expanding. Schools are asking parents to read regularly to their child and help with homework, as well as offer encouragement and concern. Is this all to the good? Could it possibly be a reaction to the lower standards to which students have been held in schools?

Is it possible that we are overlooking some negative consequences of heavier reliance on the home? Are we perhaps contributing to the wider discrepancy between the achievement of the children of the better educated and the children of the less well educated? That this may be so is suggested by the research findings that more structured, traditional teaching leads to better achievement among children of low socioeconomic status. It would appear also that systematic instruction in school does not require as much parental aid as does open, informal instruction.

Whether computers will have an overall positive effect on the learning of all children is still uncertain, but that they may contribute to the greater differences in the learning of rich and poor is more certain. Middle-class children who have one or more computers at home as well as books have a better chance at academic achievement than poorer children who have none.

Thus, as education moves out from the school to the home and community, student achievement will probably have a broader range, grade for grade. The range of achievement for each grade or age group will probably increase, and the setting of national standards will become ever more difficult. Even if all parents are encouraged to assist in their child's education and the media develop ingenious learning games for home use, parents of limited educa-

---

*It is of interest that Prince Charles, the Prince of Wales, was the first in many generations of the English royal family to be sent to school for a more democratic worldview. Those before him were tutored at home.

tion and those who have not themselves been successful learners will find it difficult to help their child with schoolwork. This is especially so for students who are in the middle grades and high school.

It would seem that the most effective way to improve achievement for all is to improve their school instruction—a solution that may, in the long run, be more effective than relying on parents to teach their children at home or to provide the technology and software for the child's advancement. If we push home schooling and parental help too far, we may well reduce a poorer child's chances for educational achievement and social mobility. Thus, we will be providing more for those who have, not for those who need help.

Television, which is part of almost every American home, has had both positive and negative effects on learning. And the effects of computers in the home are yet to be determined. What is quite clear is that the home and the media have ever greater influence on student achievement. Even home schooling, where parents take over the education of the child from the school, has been increasing. Is this beneficial for student learning? Is it good for all, or mainly for those whose parents are well educated? Does the growing involvement of parents mean that the school's responsibility is weakening? Finally, would achievement be more effectively improved by concentrating on stronger school instruction for all children?

CHAPTER 10

———

Where Do We Go from Here?
Conclusions and Recommendations

I undertook this study to find ways to improve the academic achievement of students in our elementary and high schools. There is strong agreement that students have not been achieving well. Many claim that they do less well than students did in past years (Walberg, 1997; Chall, 1997). Others claim that achievement has not declined—that, in fact, it may have improved (Berliner & Biddle, 1995). But all agree that achievement is not up to the higher levels needed in an information, high technology age—particularly among minority and poor children.

My analysis focused on teaching and learning over a period of about 100 years to determine whether the schools changed and what influence these changes might have had on academic achievement. I have also looked at the influences of the home, the community, and technology.

Because I chose to concentrate on learning and teaching does not mean that they are the only ways to improve student achievement. Indeed, research conducted during the past several decades has repeatedly focused on the importance for academic achievement of family background. The socioeconomic status of parents, their ethnicity, and their concern for learning in the home have strong effects on a child's school achievement. In the long run, other forces may be as powerful as, if not more powerful than schools in their impact on academic achievement. Indeed, the rise in the average number of years of schooling of U.S. adults from eight in the 1940s to twelve in the 1990s can be viewed as primarily an outcome of strong economic growth during these years.

My major concern, however, was with what schools can do to raise student achievement. Toward this end, I examined the relevant research evidence and the historical changes in school practices. I further concentrated on the two educational patterns that have been competing for supremacy in American schools for about a century—the classic and the progressive, the teacher-centered and student-centered.

While, in reality, schools differ in hundreds of ways, it is helpful to view them as falling into one of these two educational approaches or ideal types that have been used by anthropologists and sociologists to help them understand differences between cultures and historical periods. Ruth Benedict (1946) contrasted two cultures—an Apollonian and Dionysian—to help us understand the differences between Indian cultures in North America, and David Riesman (Riesman et al., 1955) used two types—inner-directed and other-directed, to help us understand historical changes in the American character. Following their example, I used two educational types, or approaches—the teacher-centered and the student-centered—to characterize different educational approaches.

I found these two educational approaches to have a surprising consistency. They were used in the writings of educational scholars and researchers, and in the writings of journalists, from the early 1900s through the 1990s.

I analyzed a variety of data to answer the question, Does the informal, student-centered approach lead to better school achievement than the more formal, teacher-centered? The research I examined compared achievement among matched groups of students, one of which was educated under a teacher-centered approach and the other under a student-centered approach. I also examined early descriptive reports on the effects of more formal or less formal approaches. In addition, I analyzed studies that compared student achievement in U.S. private, parochial, and public schools and also

Asian schools—which have tended to be more teacher-centered than those in the United States.

I also looked for interactions between the effects of the two educational approaches and social class, ability to learn, and school grade completed. That is, was one approach more effective for students of high or low socioeconomic status, for those who find learning relatively easy or difficult, or for those in elementary or high school?

I looked at the historical changes in the preferences for either one or the other of these approaches in schools during the past 100 years. I also relied on my experience as a teacher and researcher during the past fifty years, as well as on the experiences of my colleagues and students.

I found, from these various studies, that the traditional, teacher-centered approach generally produced higher academic achievement than the progressive, student-centered approach. Only one study reported few consistent differences in achievement between the progressive and traditional schools. But, it should be noted, none found that progressive, informal education resulted in higher academic achievement than the more formal, traditional education.

A few studies that compared the two approaches on nonacademic outcomes, such as attitude toward learning, found small differences favoring the progressive approach. But these differences were not consistent and tended to be much smaller than those found for achievement—where the traditional classes came out considerably higher in achievement than the progressive, informal ones.

Social class interacted positively with the two approaches. Indeed, whenever the students were identified as coming from families of low socioeconomic status, they achieved at higher levels when they received a more formal, traditional education. Overall, while the traditional, teacher-centered approach produced higher achievement than the progressive, student-centered approach among all students, its effects were even stronger for those students who were less well prepared.

The teacher-centered approach was also more effective for students with learning disabilities at all social levels. On the whole, the research found that at-risk students at all social levels achieved better academically when given a more traditional education. Similar results were reported recently by Jencks and Phillips (1998), who concluded that black students achieved better in traditional than in informal progressive schools.

The descriptive reports of the education of low-socioeconomic-status children, from the early 1900s to the present, noted that parents of these children voiced serious objections to having their children educated in schools that followed an informal, student-centered approach. Most preferred a traditional education for their children.

Research shows that the home characteristics that lead to good academic achievement are similar to the school characteristics that produce good achievement. Generally these home characteristics resemble traditional school characteristics, such as regularity of routines, emphasis on books, rich language, and concern for the child's academic achievement.

From the early 1900s on, American public schools have generally moved from a traditional, teacher-centered to a progressive, student-centered approach. The elite private schools and the parochial schools, however, have tended to stay with a teacher-centered approach. But even the private and parochial schools took on some of the characteristics of the student-centered schools—for example, concern with individual differences, with student growth and development, and student needs and interests. But essentially, they tended to remain more traditional when compared to most public elementary schools.

Although the student-centered schools tended to vary, most shared a greater concern than the teacher-centered schools for the psychological and social well being of individual students. There was also less concern in the student-centered schools for the systematic teaching and learning of academic skills, facts, and information.

The change from a teacher-centered to a student-centered focus was accomplished early by some schools and later by others. Rural schools tended to adopt the student-centered approach later than urban schools.

We seem to be going through a transition stage today with regard to the two approaches. There are many signs of a new interest in the traditional approach. In one year, 1996, three books on educational policy—E. D. Hirsch, Jr. (1996), Murnane and Levy (1996), and Powell (1996)—presented important data and argued forcefully for the greater effectiveness of a more traditional focus. In 1995, two of four books on education reviewed on the same day in *The New York Times Book Review* favored a traditional approach.

Other signs of interest in returning to a traditional, teacher-centered approach to education can be found in various news stories beginning in the early 1990s. One story reported that an inner-city school district, where reading scores were very low, purchased a traditional reading curriculum that had been used successfully by a private school since the early 1900s. The reading specialist in the inner city school said the children's reading scores improved with the use of this traditional program.

More recently, in a study of twenty-four schoolwide approaches to reform, the three approaches found to have the strongest evidence of effectiveness—Success for All, Direct Instruction, and High Schools That Work—all follow a traditional, teacher-centered approach. Earlier a traditional reading program for poor African American children in the elementary grades was developed by Marva Collins (1990), who claims that children do so well with it that they can read original classics from the early grades on.

The state of California has recently been undergoing a change in its reading and language arts curriculum—from a student-centered to a teacher-centered approach. "The initiative was formulated and passed after the National Assessment of Educational Progress reported that California children tied for last in the nation in fourth grade reading proficiency" (Moats, 1997, p. 1). The new reading plan calls for explicit systematic instruction in phonics and spelling as well as in comprehension, and independent reading of quality books.

Increasingly during the 1990s, high schools have been encouraging all students to take more courses in mathematics, science, and foreign languages—the traditional, harder courses (see Chapter 3, page 52).

A recent article in *The New York Review of Books* reports debates in mathematics circles between those who favor a progressive, student-centered discovery approach advocated by the National Association of Teachers of Mathematics and a more traditional approach favored by many parents and teachers (Gardner, 1998). Similar debates have been reported in science and social studies.

Together with these tangible signs that education is moving toward a more traditional, teacher-centered approach, we also find that the student-centered approach is very much alive.

There are, of course, reforms that combine features of both approaches. The most highly acclaimed, Sizer's Coalition of Essential Schools, focuses on stronger intellectual content for the high school curriculum—a teacher-centered concern (Sizer, 1983). The coalition attempts to reform high schools through greater participation and collaboration by local administrators and teachers. Yet, the coalition also has many student-centered features. It supports more open scheduling of classes to achieve greater depth, commitment, and student involvement in learning, and it relies less on standardized tests.

A few years back, I remember hearing about a young, dedicated third-grade teacher who recounted his experiences at an inner-city school committed to a whole language program. His thirty or more students were reading books of their own choosing, each on a different level. This workload put a great burden on him such that he could not sleep at night from all the pressure. He even thought of moving to a suburban school that would have fewer problem children and would offer a higher salary. But he decided to stay. In spite of his hard work, some of the children in his third grade class still could not read, and he was concerned because he did not know how to teach them. He referred the children to the school's learning disabilities specialist, whose diagnostic reports revealed that some of the children were reading below second-grade level and had unusual difficulty learning phonics.

Would these children have had a better chance if their teachers had used a more traditional approach? Based on the existing research evidence, they would most likely be farther ahead. Traditional reading instruction favors the systematic teaching of phonics and other skills in the early grades, and the research constantly finds that it leads to higher reading achievement. Thus, a more traditional reading program would have helped this dedicated teacher to meet his students' needs earlier.

Another example of the pervasiveness of student-centered education comes from a first-year teacher of seventh-grade science who reported recently having difficulty with disruptive behavior in her classes. In an interview on public radio (WBUR, March 5, 1997) she said she did all of the things that are favored by student-centered education—no textbooks; teaching groups, not the whole class; student discussions, rather than the teacher lecturing. And she made sure that the work was interesting and fun.

But the seventh graders did not seem to respond. Many did not listen and several refused to sit in their seats. Conferences with their parents did not seem to help. Then she hit on a way to have them attend and work. She had them do written work—individual written work and "book work"—instead of "hands-on" activities and discussions that seemed to encourage them not to work. She also found that she should have set definite ground rules at the very beginning of the school year so that students would know how far they could go. In reality, this beginning teacher seemed to discover, all on her own, many of the practices of traditional education—the common use of reading and writing for learning, with less focus on discovery. It is a poignant example of the damage that often results from rejecting, outright, the old for the new.

She discussed her experience with her college methods teacher, who had a different view on the matter. He believed that classroom management cannot be taught. It can only be learned on the job (cf., Barth, 1972; Delpit, 1986, 1988; Stevenson & Stigler, 1992).

The Public Agenda Foundation study cited earlier (see Ravitch, 1998) points to the persistence of student-centered characteristics in high schools. There is greater concern for "self-esteem" than for academic learning. But the students polled said they wanted a more orderly and disciplined environment for learning (Ravitch, 1998, p. 77).

There is also much ambivalence about classic and open education in the standards developed for the major subjects taught in elementary and high schools—in the national and state standards for the English language arts, mathematics, science, history, and geography. The focus of many of the standards seems to be on the process of learning (a student-centered concern) rather than on what is to be learned when (a teacher-centered concern). The national reading standards in the English language arts, for example, do not indicate the level of complexity of books that students should be able to read at different ages or grades. Nor do they specify the skills that need to be mastered at a particular age in order to make continued progress in the next grades. Instead the focus is mainly on how students are to approach their reading thoughtfully and critically from first grade onward.

The new standards for mathematics are strong on getting children to conceptualize from the beginning of first grade, but are unclear about at what point addition, subtraction, multiplication, and division should become automatic. Recently I watched a group of third-grade teachers discuss conceptual mathematics, the current approach favored for mathematics instruction. Several of the teachers said they were not sure when students should be able to compute rapidly. The head teacher said she wasn't sure either, but she insisted that her own children know basic arithmetic automatically by the third grade, as she makes them practice at home. I found it puzzling that such an important question had not been clarified in the math standards.

As can be seen, there is still considerable disagreement as to whether a traditional or a progressive approach is to be preferred. While some schools seem to be moving toward a teacher-centered emphasis, others seem to hold on to their student-centered approach and some are moving toward even stronger student-centered approaches.

I offer the following recommendations to improve academic achievement based on my various analyses.

RECOMMENDATION 1:
A GREATER EMPHASIS ON A TRADITIONAL, TEACHER-CENTERED APPROACH

Based on research, history, and experience, my first recommendation is that schools that are not already doing so put a greater emphasis on a traditional, teacher-centered education. Traditional, teacher-centered schools, according to research and practice, are more effective than progressive, student-centered schools for the academic achievement of most children. And that approach is especially beneficial for students who come to school less well prepared for academic learning—children of less educated families, inner-city children, and those with learning difficulties at all social levels.

The traditional approach has also been used successfully in remedial instruction for about 100 years. Indeed, the structure and sequencing that characterize remedial instruction in reading and math are probably the main reasons for its success. Most remedial reading programs are primarily teacher-centered in their approach. Even the most open of the remedial programs—Reading Recovery—is more effective when the teaching is more structured.

Unfortunately, the long debates about the merits and shortcomings of the two educational approaches have brought with them many widely accepted but largely untested notions. One is that traditional approaches are dull, rigid, rotelike, and disliked by students while progressive approaches are interesting, exciting, and encourage lifetime interests in learning. The evidence for such statements is scarce. And what evidence there is generally runs counter to this popular view. Stevenson and Stigler (1992) found that Japanese children who were taught using a traditional approach liked school better than U.S. children do who were taught using a progressive approach.

It is also important to realize that neither the progressive nor the traditional approach has a monopoly on good teaching. Larry Cuban calls this to our attention. Traditional and progressive schools, he notes, "differ dramatically from one another in how teachers organize their classrooms, view learning, and teach the curriculum." Can both of them be good? His answer is yes (1998, p. 48).

But the question considered here is which is better overall for academic achievement. It makes sense that a traditional approach should lead to higher achievement than a progressive approach, particularly among the less proficient students. A traditional approach makes clear to the student what the objectives are and specifies the various learning tasks to be mastered in an increasing order of difficulty. Because of this explicitness, it is of particular benefit to those who are less well prepared.

Before leaving this recommendation, it is important to note that the distinction between a progressive and a traditional approach is never pure. In practice there are variations within each approach. Because of these variations it is best to think of them as being different in emphasis. The traditional emphasis, for example, puts a greater focus on the acquisition of knowledge and skills, on books and reading materials, on grade and age standards. The progressive approach emphasizes motivation and interests, and instruction geared to individual abilities and preferences. There is less of a direct focus on facts, skills, and knowledge.

It will not be easy to bring schools from a progressive to a traditional emphasis. Lisa Delpit (1986, 1988), skillful and experienced as a progressive teacher, gave us a poignant picture of the confusion, anger, and disappointment she felt when she changed to a more traditional approach to improve the learning of her African American students.

The teachers who were highly committed to a progressive approach in the inner-city classroom described by Barth (1972) were unable to make the shift to a traditional approach. They held on to their view that traditional teaching would rob them and their students of the freedom and joy of progressive education. Further, they had not been trained as traditional teachers and knew little about how to proceed.

Most teachers have been convinced by their teacher training, professional organizations, and journals that a progressive approach is best—for a democracy and for the social and emotional well-being of the child, as well as for academic progress. Such teachers will find it difficult to look to the more structured intellectual approach of a traditional emphasis that has been held so long in low-esteem.

Even greater resistance to change will come from the long association of the educational approaches with political preferences—the student-centered with a liberal position and the teacher-centered with a conservative one.

There will need to be much rethinking and reevaluation of the two approaches by teachers and administrators. And there may also be a need for teachers and administrators to reacquaint themselves with, or to learn firsthand, the procedures associated with traditional education that lead to higher student achievement—the setting of higher academic standards, the giving and checking of homework, grading, and so on.

It will also be necessary to examine the new standards proposed by national, state, and local groups to be sure that they include guidelines not only for process but for standards on the levels that students should achieve in specific grades.

Much support will be needed by teachers and administrators. Without it we might end up greatly disappointed with the results of the teacher-centered, traditional approach. Indeed, one of the reasons often cited for the failure of progressive, student-centered education has been the inadequate training received by teachers and administrators who used it (Cremin, 1961; Goodlad, 1983). The same may happen with traditional education. Although it should be understood because of its longer historical tradition, many teachers and administrators who were trained mainly in progressive education may find it completely foreign.

Others who will need to understand the research findings of the traditional/progressive debate are textbook publishers and publishers of computer software for school and home use. Consulting firms that provide professional development courses for teachers will also need to keep up with the existing and new research in order to provide the teaching materials needed for improved achievement.

RECOMMENDATION 2:
GREATER AWARENESS OF SCIENTIFIC EVALUATION OF EDUCATION

There is a need for better uses of educational research for improving practice. From the 1900s on, the education profession has prided itself on its scientific base. The psychology of E. L. Thorndike influenced both school policy and teaching and learning in the classroom. Educational research has also been recognized and rewarded by colleges and schools of education. Faculty who conduct research are promoted faster than those who concentrate mainly on teaching. There has been a general high regard for educational research and for educational researchers.

However, there seems to be an increasing decline in the valuing and uses of educational research. In a recent book Tyack and Cuban present a series of educational changes that were implemented widely in schools but, owing to a lack of testing and research, were dropped after a few years (1995).

In various research studies I have been a part of over the past fifty years, I have found that many popular, respected practices were not supported by research. Indeed, *practice often went in a direction opposite from the existing research evidence.* Thus, while educational practice kept moving in the direction of the progressive, student-centered approaches, the research evidence kept growing in support of traditional, teacher-centered learning. This is particularly evident in beginning reading instruction. Although research evidence from the early 1900s found benefits for a structured, systematic teaching of phonics and other skills, practice went in the opposite direction—toward a progressive, student-centered approach (Chall, 1967, 1983a, 1996a).

There is also a tendency to forget earlier research findings on a particular question—to treat each study as a new phenomenon unrelated to those done earlier. Thus the early observations of the weaknesses in Dewey's Chicago Laboratory School were not taken into account later, in the planning of the Gary schools, or in the Barth open schools of the 1970s.

What explains this tendency to ignore the past educational research findings? Perhaps it is because so few in the educational profession can conduct research and interpret it. Most administrators, teachers, and curriculum specialists have little or no training in research. They must rely, then, on brief summaries and interpretations by those who know the research but who have difficulty explaining it and its relevance to teaching because of their limited classroom teaching experience.

Another reason for paying so little attention to research is the strong ideological commitments toward one or the other of the two educational approaches. Almost from the start, progressive education became "larger than life" and was viewed as *the* education that will make American children happier, more democratic, and more creative. It was difficult to question it. It seems that only scholars who had little or no connection with progressive education could oppose it. Most researchers thought twice about doing research on issues that might question the value of progressive education.

The association of the patterns with different political positions—the student-centered with the liberal and the teacher-centered with the conservative—has placed many young liberals in a difficult position. If they favor a traditional education, they fear that they will be viewed as conservative or reactionary.

Stories in newspapers and the media tend to report educational research findings in terms of debates and controversies. The relevant research evidence underlying the debates is seldom reported. Nor is any reference made to the history of the issues being debated—the two approaches' successes or failures through the years. As a result, one gets a positive, enthusiastic view of one of the positions and a critical, negative view of the other. It is quite different for reports on medical research, where the findings are presented along with the highlights of the research, important applications, and opposing views.

The tendency to omit relevant research from the past is unfortunately quite common in newspaper stories on education—and it is unfortunately not uncommon in the writings of educational researchers and curriculum specialists either. There has been a tendency to use references that are no more than five years old. Thus, in his report on the poor outcomes of open education in inner city schools, Barth makes no reference to similar findings in the Gary schools some fifty years earlier. Later, in the 1980s, Delpit made no reference to Barth's findings in the 1970s. And the proponents of whole language during the 1980s and 1990s made no reference to unfavorable findings in the progressive schools of the 1920s and 1930s.

There is also a growing tendency to express strong negative views on studies that report unexpected or unwanted findings. The sharp criticism directed at James Coleman's findings that students in private and parochial schools have higher academic achievement than matched public school students may discourage younger researchers from conducting similar research.

If we are to benefit from educational research, schools of education may have to provide teachers and administrators with a better understanding of educational research. We have to give serious consideration to how much practitioners need to know about research. Surely they need to understand enough of it to benefit from it in their practice. Unless the research is understood by those who ultimately use it, it has very limited value for practice.

Further, we must have some agreement as to what constitutes "enough research evidence" on an issue to conclude for or against a practice. If we do not have some understanding of what constitutes enough evidence for "best practices," we will continue to exhaust (and perhaps demoralize) ourselves studying the same questions over and over again. This, in a sense, is what has happened with the research on reading instruction in the early grades. From the first-grade U.S. Office of Education studies by Bond and Dykstra (1967) to the research reviews by Chall (1967, 1983a, 1996a), Anderson, Hiebert, Scott, and Wilkinson (1985), Adams (1990), and most recently the National Research Council study by Snow et al. (1998), the findings and conclusions were essentially the same—that systematic instruction in phonics leads to better results.

In spite of the extensive evidence since the early 1900s, it is only perhaps recently that it has been given sufficient attention. A frequent explanation was that the evidence was not adequate (see Carbo, 1988; Honig, 1996). However, when many school systems suffered a loss in early reading achievement in the 1990s, they turned to the skills that they had rejected earlier, explaining that now it was all right to do so because we now have sufficient evidence of its value. But the evidence existed from a much earlier date.

SOME CONCLUDING THOUGHTS ON THE USES OF THE FINDINGS IN THIS BOOK

The major conclusion of my study in this book is that a traditional, teacher-centered approach to education generally results in higher academic achievement than a progressive, student-centered approach. This is particularly so among students who are less well prepared for academic learning—poor children and those with learning difficulties at all social and economic levels.

Are these conclusions also applicable to students of all ages and grade levels and for all subjects—reading, math, science, and social studies? These questions are more difficult to answer from the research evidence. Although there are quantitative studies at both the elementary and high school levels, the great majority are at the elementary grades. However, in spite of the differences in numbers, the outcomes are generally the same—an advantage for achievement of the traditional approach in both elementary and high school. But there are a few signs in the research that the advantage of the traditional, teacher-centered approach is less in high school than in elementary school. This is suggested by the Eight-Year Study of high school students, which found no significant differences between a progressive or a traditional approach. But the small differences that were found seemed to favor the progressive, student-centered approach.

As research evidence becomes available, we may well find that each approach has some advantage for academic achievement at different levels of education and proficiency. We may find that the traditional approach is more effective for beginners who first acquire knowledge and skills. Then, as they move beyond the basics, a progressive approach may prove more effective (see Chall, 1983b, 1996b; Hendley, 1986).

Thus, while the present research evidence suggests that a traditional approach leads to better academic achievement at all levels, additional research may find that a progressive approach may be more effective than the traditional at higher levels of education.

Another objection that has been raised is that, since the traditional approach tends to focus on knowledge and skills—which tend to be measured by most standardized achievement tests—it has an advantage on such tests when compared to a progressive approach. This may well be. But it should be noted that our evidence for the greater effectiveness of teacher-centered education comes from data other than standardized tests alone. We should also remember that those who have constructed standardized tests have early on included items on higher-order thinking. Thus, E. L. Thorndike, in his "Reading as Reasoning" (1917), noted that at least one-third of the questions on his reading tests for the intermediate grades assessed the ability to reason.

Finally, is it realistic to reject the results of tests that measure knowledge and skills that are well established to be necessary for progress in the higher educational goals of reasoning and problem solving (see Gardner & Boix-Mansilla, 1994)?

Based on the existing evidence—the qualitative, quantitative, and historical evidence—the achievement effects of traditional education appear to be stronger than those of progressive education. This is particularly so for those students who are still acquiring essential knowledge and basic skills and for those who lag behind for various reasons.

Others may still have concerns about classifying the two approaches. Indeed, the existence of "hybrids" that claim to follow one approach, but which have many of the characteristics of the other, seems to be quite common (Cuban, 1993; Tyack & Cuban, 1995). It is therefore suggested that the approaches be viewed as having a given emphasis—a progressive or a traditional emphasis. We should also note that these approaches, whether called traditional or progressive, teacher-centered or student-centered, old or new, have been with us for most of the past century. And whether one leads to better academic achievement than the other seems to be as fresh an issue today as it was 100 years ago.

As noted earlier, programs identified as effective for schoolwide reform have been strong, structured instructional programs that specify the skills and knowledge to be acquired, and use frequent assessment (Herman et al., 1999).

It is also of interest that, while each program is designed for all children, it is recommended especially for those who have low-socioeconomic-status backgrounds and those who have difficulty in learning.

Also in 1999, *The New York Times* (Gershenson, 1999) carried an article on an experimental school in New York City that uses a progressive, student-centered approach and emphasizes the arts. Recent statewide tests found that the students were achieving low reading scores. The position of the school—so reminiscent of the progressive schools of the past—was that "young children develop at their own pace, and should not be intellectually rushed."

The parents also defended the school program, saying they do not want their children "flooded with information." Instead, they prefer to have them sing and dance and being happy. One mother said she wanted the school to "educate the entire person, instead of just shoving them full of knowledge they cannot use and have no outlet for."

And so we seem to be ending where we began in the early 1900s. The research evidence shows that a traditional, teacher-centered emphasis is best for academic achievement, yet many schools and parents continue to favor a progressive, student-centered emphasis.

Hopefully, the current emphasis on raising academic standards, together with the strong research evidence on the comparative effectiveness of teacher-centered approaches, will bring more schools to reevaluate their programs and make the needed changes.

Appendix

KEY DIFFERENCES BETWEEN TEACHER-CENTERED AND STUDENT-CENTERED INSTRUCTION

What Should Be Learned in School?

Teacher-Centered

Knowledge from the past, present, and foreseeable future; skills important for the individual and society. A core curriculum based on the traditional disciplines of reading, writing, literature, mathematics, science, social studies, and art—arranged in an increasing order of difficulty.

Student-Centered

School learning should be based on the learner's interests and needs. Theoretically there is no required core curriculum that is arranged hierarchically. Subject matter is not structured. The emphasis is on the learning process and on a variety of subjects that are integrated to make them more meaningful.

What Should Be Emphasized—Product or Process?

Teacher-Centered

Emphasis is on learning content and skills. Thinking and problem solving are learned with content.

Student-Centered

Emphasis is on process and on how to solve problems—how to think. The content is less important than the process.

Specific versus Integrated Content

Teacher-Centered

There is a tendency to teach the traditional subjects (i.e., reading, writing, spelling, social studies, science) separately in the elementary grades. There may be some integration, but not until after the basics of the separate subjects have been acquired.

Student-Centered

There is a preference for integrating subjects: reading, writing, spelling, literature, speaking, and listening into language arts; history and geography into social studies; and more recently social studies with reading and writing, and writing and science with literature.

What Should the Curriculum Be?

Teacher-Centered

With a focus on basic skills, the traditional curriculum has changed little in the elementary grades since the early 1800s.

The traditional subjects—reading, writing, spelling and math—are taught separately in the early grades instead of being combined into language arts or whole language. History, geography, and science are usually taught separately in the middle grades.

Student-Centered

There is much variation in what is taught and when it is taught.

Theoretically, any subject can serve to develop problem-solving abilities and creativity. There is less hierarchy of subject matter. Reading, writing, spelling, and literature are usually combined. Social studies combines history, geography, sociology, and anthropology.

How Students Are Perceived

Teacher-Centered

Students are expected to learn what is taught. What is taught should be as interesting as possible, but it is selected because it fits in with an overall hierarchy of learning tasks.

The student comes to school with both good and questionable habits and attitudes. Schools are designed to "humanize" him or her into being a good citizen and good learner.

Student-Centered

Ideally, the best learning comes when students are interested in what they learn. Therefore, teachers are to encourage students to follow their own interests in their learning.

Students are assumed to have good attitudes and habits and to naturally want to learn and become good citizens.

Moral Development

Teacher-Centered

Students learn right from wrong from their studies and from extra curricular activities.

Student-Centered

Moral behavior develops from the individual's experience. It is best learned when not taught directly.

Standards and Assessment

Teacher-Centered

Formal and informal tests are given to determine the student's aptitude for and mastery of the subject matter that has been taught—the content and the skills.

Contemporary teacher-centered schools make use of standardized tests of aptitude and achievement.

Student-Centered

There is an ambivalence about both standards and assessments. Standards are problematic because of the great emphasis on individual differences.

There is a preference for qualitative and diagnostic tests and, more recently, for portfolios.

Attitudes toward Individual Differences

Teacher-Centered

All students are expected to learn the basic skills (reading, writing, math) and the traditional content subjects (history, geography, and science) as their aptitude permits. While individual differences in ability are recognized, all who attend school are expected to reach at least some minimal standards in knowledge and skills.

Student-Centered

Student learning is expected to vary by interests, motivation, and ability. Therefore, not all are held to the same standards. Also, because of the knowledge explosion, students cannot be expected to learn all there might be to learn. Therefore, they should learn, not subjects, but how to learn, think, and solve problems; and they should know how to find what they need when they need it.

Optimum Level of Difficulty for Learning

Teacher-Centered

The tendency is to prefer more-difficult rather than easier instructional tasks and materials.

Student-Centered

The tendency is to prefer easier tasks and materials because students are expected to do much of their learning independently.

Grading/Report Cards

Teacher-Centered

Letter and/or percentage grades are given for most subjects. Sometimes scores from standardized achievement tests are also included on the report cards received by parents.

Student-Centered

Oral reports directed to the parent are considered the ideal form of reporting pupil progress. A written report in narrative form may also be used.

Promotion

Teacher-Centered

Promotion is largely by achievement. If the achievement is thought to be too low for success in subsequent grades, the student may be retained for a year. Usually a student is retained twice, at most, in the elementary grades.

Student-Centered

Social promotion is preferred. The student is promoted with his age group even if his achievement is quite low. It is assumed that the student will benefit from predictable promotion since ideally the instruction is matched to the student's instructional level, not to his or her grade placement. Also, to hold back a student is considered questionable for his or her self-esteem.

Attitude toward Use of Textbooks and Other Teaching Materials

Teacher-Centered

Textbooks are important to assure minimal coverage of content. Additional materials are recommended as well, for example, encyclopedias and other reference works, books, newspapers, and magazines, and more recently computer programs.

Student-Centered

Original sources—for example, children's literature, novels, historical works, original documents, and more recently computers—are preferred to textbooks. Textbooks are not preferred because they are considered dull and not geared to the individual needs and interests of students. For science, hands-on experiences are preferred to reading materials.

How Students Difficulties
Are Explained and Treated

Teacher-Centered

The emphasis is on learning and teaching. If the student is failing, the tendency is to look into what he or she has not learned and how it can be provided by the school. Behavioral and emotional problems are also recognized as possible causes of learning difficulties. But there is a greater emphasis on treating academic difficulties directly, even if the causes are nonacademic.

Student-Centered

The cause for academic difficulties is usually sought in noneducational factors—lack of motivation, emotional problems, or a troubled or dysfunctional home. For students in first grade, a lack of progress is often stated in terms of lack of readiness for schooling.

Discipline

Teacher-Centered

Rules of behavior are made explicit, are taught, and appropriate steps are taken when a child or class does not follow them.

Student-Centered

Discipline is seldom discussed. It is assumed that curriculum and methods that are child-centered and based on the child's ability will minimize the need for discipline. Rules of behavior are usually not made explicit.

What Is the Teacher's Educational Background?

Teacher-Centered

Education in the subject matter being taught is preferred, especially for high school teachers. There is less concern with the teacher's knowledge of methods of teaching than with knowledge and expertise in the specific subject matter.

Student-Centered

The teacher's mastery of subject matter is considered less important than an understanding of child and adolescent development, and how to stimulate and encourage students' creativity and self-expression.

Should Schools Focus on Affect and Motivation or Knowledge and the Intellect?

Teacher-Centered

The emphasis of the school should be on the intellect—on academic learning. This does not mean that motivation and affect are ignored; it means that the major focus of schools should be on academic learning, and that motivation and affect are important only as they influence academic learning.

Student-Centered

The emphasis is on affect and motivation, with less emphasis on the content of what is learned. In order for students to be motivated to learn math and science, certain programs may be preferred because students find them more interesting and exciting.

References

ABT Associates. (1977). *Education as experimentation: A planned variation model: Vol. IV-B. Effects of follow-through models.* Cambridge, MA: ABT Books.

Adams, M. (1990). *Beginning to read: Thinking and learning about print.* Cambridge, MA: MIT Press.

Adams, G. L., & Engleman, S. (1996). *Research on direct instruction: 25 years beyond Distar.* Seattle, WA: Educational Achievement Systems.

Alkin, M. C. (Ed.). (1992). *The Encyclopedia of Educational Research* (6th ed.). New York: Macmillan.

Anderson, R. C., Hiebert, E. H., Scott, J. A., & Wilkinson, I. A. G. (1985). *Becoming a nation of readers: The report of the Commission on Reading.* Champaign, IL: Center for the Study of Reading and the National Academy of Education.

Angus, D., & Mirel, J. (1995). Rhetoric and reality: The high school curriculum. In D. Ravitch & M. A. Vinovskis (Eds.), *Learning from the past: What history teaches us about school reform* (pp. 295–328). Baltimore: Johns Hopkins University Press.

Barth, R. S. (1972). *Open education and the American school.* New York: Agathon Press.

Benedict, R. (1946). *Patterns of culture.* New York: Penguin Books.

Bennett, N. (1976). *Teaching styles and pupil progress.* Cambridge, MA: Harvard University Press.

Bestor, A. (1985). *Educational wastelands: The retreat from learning in our public schools* (2nd ed.). Urbana: University of Illinois Press. (First edition published 1953)

Berliner, D. C., & Biddle, B. J. (1995). *The manufactured crisis: Myths, fraud, and the attack on American public schools.* Reading, MA: Addison-Wesley.

Bloom, A. (1987). *The closing of the American mind: How higher education has failed democracy and impoverished the souls of today's students.* New York: Simon & Schuster.

Bloom, B. (Ed.). (1985). *Developing talent in young children.* New York: Ballantine Books.

Bloom, B., & Sosniak, L. A. (1981). Talent development vs. schooling. *Educational Leadership, 39*(2), 86–95.

Bond, G. L., & Dykstra, R. (1967). *Coordinating Center for First Grade Reading Instruction Programs* (Final Report of Project No. x-001, Contact No. OE-5-10-264). Minneapolis: University of Minnesota.

Bourne, R. S. (1970). *The Gary schools*. Cambridge, MA: MIT Press.

Bryk, A. S., Lee, V. E., & Holland, P. B. (1993). *Catholic schools and the common good*. Cambridge, MA: Harvard University Press.

Butts, D. P. (1982). Science education. In H. E. Mitzel (Ed.), *The encyclopedia of educational research, Vol. 4* (5th ed., pp. 1665–1675). New York: Free Press.

Carbo, M. (1988). Debunking the great phonics myth. *Phi Delta Kappan, 70,* 226–240.

Carr, E. R., Wesley, E. B., & Murra, W. F. (1950). Social studies. In W. S. Monroe (Ed.), *The encyclopedia of educational research* (pp. 1213–1238). New York: Macmillan.

Chall, J. S. (1958). *Readability: An appraisal of research and application*. Columbus: Ohio State University Press.

Chall, J. S. (Ed.). (1963, 1964). *Folktales of other lands* (8 vols.). New York: Bobbs Merrill.

Chall, J. S. (1967). *Learning to read: The great debate*. New York: McGraw Hill.

Chall, J. S. (1983a). *Learning to read: The great debate* (2nd ed.). New York: McGraw Hill.

Chall, J. S. (1983b). *Stages of reading development*. New York: McGraw Hill.

Chall, J. S. (1987). The importance of instruction in reading methods for all teachers. In R. Bowler (Ed.), *Intimacy with language: A forgotten basic in teacher education* (pp. 15–23). Baltimore: Orton Dyslexia Society.

Chall, J. S. (1989). Could the decline be real? Recent trends in reading instruction and support in the U.S. *Report of the NAEP Technical Review Panel on the 1986 reading anomaly, the accuracy of NAEP trends, and issues raised by state-level NAEP comparisons.* Washington, DC: Center for Education Statistics and U.S. Department of Education.

Chall, J. S. (1991, Fall). *Review of early literacy: The developing child* by Joan Brooks McLane & Gilligan Dowley McNamee. *Teachers College Record, 93*(1), 174–177.

Chall, J. S. (1992, Winter). The new reading debates: Evidence from science, art and ideology. *Teachers College Record, 94*(2), 315–328.

Chall, J. S. (1992–1993, December/January). Research supports direct instruction models. *Reading Today,* pp. 8–10.

Chall, J. S. (Ed.). (1994). *Classic American readers* (6 vols.). Kansas City: Andrews & McMeel.

Chall, J. S. (1996a). *Learning to read: The great debate* (3rd ed.). Fort Worth, TX: Harcourt Brace.

Chall, J. S. (1996b). *Stages of reading development* (2nd ed.). Fort Worth, TX: Harcourt Brace.

Chall, J. S. (1997). American reading achievement: Should we worry? *Research in English, 30*(3), 328–434.

Chall, J. S. (1999). Some thoughts on reading research: Revisiting the first-grade studies. *Reading Research Quarterly, 34(1)*, 8–10.

Chall, J. S., Bissex, G., Conard, S., & Harris-Sharples, S. (1996). *Qualitative assessment of text difficulty: A practical guide for teachers and writers*. Cambridge, MA: Brookline Books.

Chall, J. S., & Conard, S. S. (1991). *Should textbooks challenge students? The case for easier or harder books*. New York: Teachers College Press.

Chall, J. S., Conard, S. S., & Harris, S. H. (1977). *An analysis of textbooks in relation to declining SAT scores*. Prepared for the Advisory Panel on the Scholastic Aptitude Test Score Decline, jointly sponsored by the College Board and Educational Testing Service.

Chall, J. S., & Curtis, M. E. (1991). Children at risk. In J. Flood, J. Jensen, D. Lapp, & J. R. Squire (Eds.), *The handbook of research in the teaching of the English language arts* (pp. 349–355). Newark, DE: International Reading Association and National Council of Teachers of English.

Chall, J. S., & Dale, E. (1995a). *Readability revisited and the new Dale–Chall readability formula*. Cambridge, MA: Brookline Books.

Chall, J. S., & Dale, E. (1995b). *Manual for the new Dale–Chall readability formula*. Cambridge, MA: Brookline Books.

Chall, J. S., & Feldmann, S. (1966). First grade reading: An analysis of the interactions of professed methods, teacher implementation and child background. *The Reading Teacher, 19*, 569–575.

Chall, J. S., Jacobs, V. A., & Baldwin, L. E. (1990). *The reading crisis: Why poor children fall behind*. Cambridge, MA: Harvard University Press.

Chall, J. S., & Peterson, R. W. (1986). The influence of neuroscience upon educational practice. In S. L. Friedman, K. A. Klivington, & R. W. Peterson (Eds.), *The brain, cognition, and education* (pp. 287–318). Orlando, FL: Academic Press.

Cheney, L. (1997, July 20). Editorial column. *The New York Times*, p. E15.

Cohen, R. D. (1990). *Children of the mill: Schooling and society in Gary, Indiana 1906–1960*. Bloomington: Indiana University Press.

Coleman, J. S., Campbell, E., Hobson, C., McPartland, J., Mood, A., Weinfield, F., & York, R. (1966). *Equality of educational opportunity*. Washington, DC: U.S. Government Printing Office.

Coleman, J. S., & Hoffer, T. (1987). *Public and private high schools: The impact of communities*. New York: Basic Books.

Collins, M. (1990). *Marva Collins' way* (2nd ed.). Los Angeles: Tarcher.

Crabtree, C. (1992). Social studies education, elementary schools. In M. C. Alkin (Ed.), *The encyclopedia of educational research, Vol. 4* (6th ed., pp. 1229–1238). New York: Macmillan.

Cremin, L. (1961). *The transformation of the school*. New York: Knopf.

Cremin, L. (1988). *American education: The metropolitan experience 1876–1980*. New York: Harper & Row.

Cuban, L. (1990, January). Reforming, again, again, and again. *Educational Researcher, 19*(1), pp. 3–13.

Cuban, L. (1993). How *teachers taught: Constancy and change in American classrooms, 1890–1990*. New York: Teachers College Press.

Cuban, L. (1998). How progressives and traditionalists undermine our understanding of what is "good" in schools. *Education Week, 17*(20), 33, 48.

Curtis, M. E. (1986). *The National Assessment of Reading: Past and future directions*. Commissioned by the Study Group on the National Assessment of Student Achievement; Appendix B of *The nation's report card*, by the National Assessment of Educational Progress.

Delpit, L. D. (1986). Minority view: Skills and other dilemmas of a progressive black educator. *Harvard Educational Review, 56*(4), 379–385.

Delpit, L. D. (1988). The silenced dialogue: Power and pedagogy in educating other people's children. *Harvard Educational Review, 58*(3), 280–298.

Delpit, L. D. (1995). *Other people's children: Cultural conflict in the classroom*. New York: New Press.

Dewey, J. (1900). The *school and society*. Chicago: University of Chicago Press.

Dewey, J. (1938). *Experience and education*. New York: Macmillan.

Durkin, D. (1966). *Children who read early*. New York: Teachers College Press.

Durkin, D. (1974–1975). A six-year study of children who learned to read in school at the age of four. *Reading Research Quarterly, 10*, 9–61.

Edmonds, R. (1979). Effective schools for the urban poor. *Educational Leadership, 37*, 15–30.

Elmore, R. F. (1995, August). Teaching, learning and school organization: Principles of practice and the regularities of schooling. *Educational Administration Quarterly, 31*(3), 355–374.

Eppenstein, J. M. (1966, May). *Efforts to teach reading to the culturally deprived child throughout history*. Unpublished seminar paper for selected problems in the teaching of the language arts. Harvard Graduate School of Education, Cambridge, MA.

Featherstone, J. (1971a). Open Schools I: The British and the U.S. *The New Republic, 165*(11), 20–23.

Featherstone, J. (1971b). Open Schools II: Tempering a fad. *The New Republic, 165*(13), 17–21.

Feitelson, D. (1988). *Facts and fads in beginning reading*. Norwood, NJ: Ablex.

Fey, J. T. (1982). Mathematics education. In H. E. Mitzel (Ed.), *The encyclopedia of educational research, Vol. 3* (5th ed., pp. 1166–1180). New York: Free Press.

Flesch, R. (1955). *Why Johnny can't read*. New York: Harper & Row.

Flexner, A., & Bachman, F. P. (1970). Epilogue. In R. S. Bourne, *The Gary schools* (pp. 205–287). Cambridge, MA: MIT Press.

Fraley, A. (1981). *Schooling and innovation*. New York: Tyler Gibson.

Fuson, K. C. (1992). Mathematics education, elementary. In M. C. Alkin (Ed.), *The encyclopedia of educational research, Vol. 3* (6th ed., pp. 776–785). New York: Macmillan.

Gage, N. L. (1978). *The scientific basis of the art of teaching*. New York: Teachers College Press.

Gage, N. L., & Berliner, D. C. (1992). *Educational psychology* (5th ed.). Boston: Houghton Mifflin.

Gardner, H., & Boix-Mansilla, V. (1994, Winter). Teaching for understanding in the disciplines—and beyond. *Teachers College Record, 96*(2), 198–218.

Gardner, M. (1998, September 24). The new new math. *The New York Review of Books,* pp. 9–12.

Gates, A. I. (1937). The necessary mental age for beginning reading. *Elementary School Journal, 37,* 497–508.

Gershenson, A. (1999, March 20). Experimental school in jeopardy. *New York Times,* p. B4.

Gesell, A. L., Ilg, F. L., & Ames, L. B. (1956). *Youth: The years from ten to sixteen.* New York: Harper.

Good, T. L., & Brophy, J. E. (1987). *Looking in classrooms.* New York: Harper & Row.

Goodlad, J. I. (1983). *A place called school: Prospects for the future.* New York: McGraw-Hill.

Graham, P. A. (1999, January 27). Delineating the boundaries of a people's aspiration: Our rhetoric of educational access has often belied a contradictory reality. *Education Week,* 44–45, 50.

Hall, G. S. (1901). The ideal school as based on child study. *Forum, 32*(24).

Hall, G. S. (1911). *Educational problems* (Vol. 2). New York: Appleton.

Harris, A. J. (1940). *How to increase reading ability: A guide to diagnostic and remedial methods.* New York: Longmans, Green.

Hayes, D., Wolfer, L., & Wolfe, M. (1993). *Was the decline in SAT scores caused by simplified school texts?* Paper presented at the annual meeting of the American Sociological Association, Miami, FL.

Hayes, R. B., & Wuerst, R. C. (1969). *Four instructional approaches to beginning reading—three years later.* Paper presented at the convention of the International Reading Association, Boston, MA. (ERIC Document Reproduction Service No. ED 020098)

Hendley, B. P. (1986). *Dewey, Russell, Whitehead: Philosophers as educators.* Carbondale & Edwardsville: Southern Illinois University Press.

Herman, R., Aladjem, D., Smith-O'Malley, A., McMahon, P., Quinones, S., Masem, E., Reeve, A., Mulligan, I., & Woodruff, D. (1999). *An educators' guide to schoolwide reform.* Arlington, VA: Educational Research Service.

Hersey, J. (1954, May 24). Why do students bog down on first R? *Life Magazine, 36,* 136–140.

Hirsch, E. D., Jr. (1987). *Cultural literacy: What every American needs to know.* Boston, MA: Houghton Mifflin Company.

Hirsch, E. D., Jr. (1996). *The schools we need and why we don't have them.* New York: Doubleday.

Hoff, D. J. (1998, November 4). Math Council again mulling its standards: Proposals include more basic skills. *Education Week, 58*(10), 1–18.

Hoffman, J. V., McCarthey, S., Abbott, J., Christian, C., Corman, L., Curry, C., Dressman, M., Elliot, B., Matherne, D., & Stahl, D. (1993). *Basal reader systems: An analysis of recent developments and trends at the first-grade level*. Austin, TX: University of Texas.

Honig, B. (1996). *How should we teach our children to read?* For Far West Laboratory for Educational Research and Development. Thousand Oaks, CA: Corwin Press.

House, E. R., Glass, G. V., McLean, L. D., & Walker, D. F. (1978, March). Critiquing a follow through evaluation. *Phi Delta Kappan, 59*(7), 473–474.

Huey, E. B. (1908). *The psychology and pedagogy of reading*. New York: Macmillan.

Hutchins, R. M. (1970). The conflict in education. In H. Ozmon (Ed.), *Contemporary critics of education*. Danville, IL: Interstate Printers & Publishers.

Jackson, J. (1977, January). The PUSH for Excellence in big-city schools. *Phi Delta Kappan, 58*(5), 383–388.

Jackson, P. W. (1986). *The practice of teaching*. New York: Teachers College Press.

Jacobs, J. (1992). *Systems of survival: A dialogue on the moral foundations of commerce and politics*. New York: Random House.

Jansky, J., & de Hirsch, K. (1972). *Preventing reading failure: Prediction, diagnosis, intervention*. New York: Harper & Row.

Jencks, C., & Phillips, M. (1998, September 30). The black–white test score gap. *Education* Week, *18*(4), 44.

Kellaghan, T., Sloane, K., Alvarez, B., & Bloom, B. S. (1993). *The home environment and school learning: Promoting parental involvement in the education of children*. San Francisco: Jossey-Bass.

Kennedy, M. M. (1978). Findings from the follow through planned variation study. *Educational Researcher, 7*(6), 3–11.

Kristsol, I. (1995). *Neoconservatism: The autobiography of an idea*. New York: Free Press.

Lagemann, E. (1989). The plural worlds of educational research. *History of Education Quarterly, 29*(2), 183–214.

Levin, H. M. (1995). Learning from Accelerated Schools. In J. H. Block, S. T. Everson, & T. R. Guskey (Eds.), *School improvement programs*. New York: Scholastic Books.

Levine, A., & Levine, F. P. (1970). Introduction. In R. S. Bourne, *The Gary schools* (pp. xii–lv). Cambridge, MA: MIT Press.

Mann, D., & Lawrence, J. (1980–1981). Introduction to *Impact on instructional improvement: Instructionally effective schools*. A publication of the New York State Association for Supervision and Curriculum Development, *16*(4), 5–10.

Mathews, M. M. (1966). *Teaching to read: Historically considered*. Chicago: The University of Chicago Press.

McGrath, E. (1981, November). Pricklies vs. Gooeys: Conflicting theories of learning in the wake of Head Start. *Time, 118*(19), 107.

McLane, J. B., & McNamee, G. D. (1990). *Early literacy: The developing child*. Cambridge, MA: Harvard University Press.

Mead, M. (1964). *The school in American culture*. Cambridge, MA: Harvard University Press. (The Inglis Lecture, delivered March 15, 1950, Harvard University)

Mitzel, H. E. (Ed.). (1982). *The encyclopedia of educational research* (5th ed.). New York: Free Press.

Moats, L. C. (1997). California Reading Initiative: A revolution in education policy. *Perspectives* (Newsletter of the Orton Dyslexia Society), *23*(4), 1–5.

Monroe, M. (Ed.). (1932). *Children who cannot read*. Chicago: University of Chicago Press.

Monroe, W. S. (Ed.). (1950). *The encyclopedia of educational research* (rev. ed.). New York: Macmillan.

Morphett, M. V., & Washburne, C. (1931). When do school children begin to read? *Elementary School Journal, 31*, 496–503.

Mullis, I. V. S., Campbell, J. R., & Farstrup, A. E. (1993). *NAEP 1992 reading report card for the nation and the* states. Washington, DC: National Center for Educational Statistics, U.S. Department of Education.

Mullis, I. V. S., & Jenkins, L. B. (1990). *The reading report card, 1971–1988: Trends from the nation's report card*. Princeton, NJ: Educational Testing and National Assessment of Educational Progress.

Murnane, R., & Levy, F. (1996). *Teaching the new basic skills: Principles for educating children to thrive in a changing economy*. New York: Free Press.

National Assessment of Educational Progress (NAEP). (1971). *Reading report card*. Princeton, NJ: Educational Testing Service.

Neill, A. S. (1960). *Summerhill: A radical approach to child rearing*. New York: Hart Publications.

National Association of Educational Progress. (October, 1996). *Reading proficiency and home support for literacy*. Washington, DC: National Center for Educational Statistics (NCES), Report No. 96-814.

National Commission on Excellence in Education. (1983). *A nation at risk: The imperative for educational reform*. Washington, DC: U.S. Department of Education.

Ohio State University. (1940). *Eight year study: A report of the Ohio State University to the Commission on the Relation of School and College of the Progressive Education Association*. Columbus: Ohio State University Press.

Olson, L. (1999, February 17). Researchers rate whole-school reform models. *Education* Week, *18*(23), 1, 14–15.

Olson, S. (1998, September 30). Science friction. *Education Week, 18*(4), 24–29.

Orton, S. T. (1937). *Reading, writing and speech problems in children*. New York: Norton.

Papert, S. (1996). The *connected family: Bridging the digital generation gap*. Atlanta: Longstreet Press.

Perfetti, C. A. (1985). *Reading ability*. New York: Oxford University Press.

Piaget, J. (1970). *Structuralism*. New York: Basic Books.

Ponder, G., & Davis, 0. L., Jr. (1982). Social studies education. In H. E. Mitzel (Ed.), *The encyclopedia of educational research, Vol. 4*. New York: Free Press.

Popp, H. M. (1975). Current practices in the teaching of beginning reading. In J. B. Carroll & J. S. Chall (Eds.), *Toward a literate society*, (pp. 101–146). New York: McGraw-Hill.

Powell, A. G. (1996). *Lessons from privilege: The American prep school tradition*. Cambridge, MA: Harvard University Press.

Powers, S. R. (1950). Science education. In W. S. Monroe (Ed.), *The encyclopedia of educational research* (pp. 1133–1144). New York: Macmillan.

Rath, L. K. (1990). *Phonemic awareness: Its role in reading development*. Unpublished manuscript, Harvard University Graduate School of Education, Cambridge, MA.

Ravitch, D. (1983). *The troubled crusade: American education, 1945–1980*. New York: Basic Books.

Ravitch, D. (1998). What do teenagers want? *Selected readings on School Reform, 2*(1), 77. (Original work published in *Forbes*, October 20, 1997)

Read, C., & Ruyter, L. (1985). Reading and spelling skills in adults of low literacy. *Remedial and Special Education, 6*(6), 43–52.

Resnick, L. B., Klopfer, L. E., & Leopold E. (Eds.). (1989). *Toward the thinking curriculum: Current cognitive research.* 1989 yearbook of the Association for Supervision and Curriculum Development.

Rickover, H. G. (1970). Education and freedom. In H. Ozmon (Ed.), *Contemporary critics of education*. Danville, IL: Interstate Printers & Publishers.

Riesman, D., Glazer, N., & Denney, R. (1955). *The lonely crowd*. New York: Doubleday Anchor Books.

Rodriguez, R. (1982). *Hunger of memory: The education of Richard Rodriguez, an autobiography*. Boston, MA: Goodine.

Rosenak, M. (1987). *Commandments and concerns: Jewish religious education in secular society*. New York: Jewish Publication Society.

Rosenshine, B. (1976). Classroom instruction. In N. L. Gage (Ed.), *The psychology of teaching methods*. Seventy-fifth yearbook of the National Society for the Study of Education (pp. 335–371). Chicago: University of Chicago Press.

Rosenshine, B. V. (1987). Explicit teaching. In B. D. Berliner & B. V. Rosenshine (Eds.), *Talks to teachers: A festschrift for N. L. Gage* (pp. 75–92). New York: Random House.

Rosenshine, B., & Meister, C. (1994). Scaffolds for teaching higher order cognitive-level strategies. Unpublished paper. (See also the earlier version: Rosenshine & Meister [1992] in *Educational Leadership, 49*[7], 26–33)

Rothenberg, J. (1989). The open classroom reconsidered. *Elementary School Journal, 90*(1), 69—86.

Rowe, M. B. (1992). Science education, elementary schools. In M. C. Alkin (Ed.), *The encyclopedia of educational research, Vol. 4* (6th ed., pp. 1172–1176). New York: Macmillan.

Ruenzel, D. (1995, April, 19). Two schools of thought. *Teachers Magazine*, pp. 23–29.

Rusk, R. R., & Scotland, J. (1979). *Doctrines of the great educators* (5th ed.). New York: St. Martin's Press.

Rutter, M., Maughan, B., Mortimer, P., & Ouston, J., with Smith, A. (1979). *Fifteen thousand hours: Secondary schools and their effects on children*. Cambridge, MA: Harvard University Press.

Samuels, J. S. (1988). Characteristics of exemplary reading programs. In J. S. Samuels & P. D. Pearson (Eds.), *Changing school reading programs: Principles and case studies*. Newark, DE: International Reading Association.

Shepard, L. (1989, March). How best to protect children from inappropriate school expectations, practices, and policies. *Young Children, 44*(3), 14–24.

Silberman, C. E. (1970). *Crisis in the classroom*. New York: Random House.

Sizer, T. R. (1983). High school reform: The need for engineering. *Phi Delta Kappan, 64*(10), 679–683.

Slavin, R. E. (1992). *Success for all: A relentless approach to prevention and early intervention in elementary schools*. Arlington, VA: Educational Research Service.

Smith, M. (1949). *And madly teach: A layman looks at public education*. Chicago: Henry Regnery Co.

Snow, C. E., Burns, M. S., & Griffin, P. (Eds.). (1998). *Preventing reading difficulties in young children*. Washington, DC: National Academy Press.

Stallings, J. (1975). Implementation and child effects of teaching practices in follow through classrooms. *Monographs of the Society for Research in Child Development, 40*(7–8), Serial No. 103.

Stanovich, K. E. (1986). Matthew effects in reading: Some consequences of individual differences in the acquisition of literacy. *Reading Research Quarterly, 21*, 360–407.

Stanovich, K. (1991). Word recognition: Changing perceptions. In R. Barr, M. L. Kamil, P. Rbsenthal, & P. D. Pearson (Eds.), *Handbook of reading research, Vol. 2* (pp. 418–452). New York: Longman.

Steinberg, L., with Bradford, B., & Dornbusch, S. M. (1996). *Beyond the classroom: Why school reform has failed and what parents need to do*. New York: Simon & Schuster.

Stevens, R., & Rosenshine, B. (1981). Advances in research on teaching. *Exceptional Education Quarterly, 2*(I), 1–9.

Stevenson, H., & Stigler, J. (1992). *The learning gap: Why our schools are failing and what we can learn from Japanese and Chinese education*. New York: Simon & Schuster.

Strucker, J. D. (1995). *Patterns of reading in adult basic education*. Unpublished doctoral dissertation, Harvard University Graduate School of Education, Gutman Library.

Thorndike, E. L. (1917). Reading as reasoning: A study of mistakes in paragraph reading. *Journal of Educational Psychology, 8*, 323–332.

Thorndike, R. L. (1973). *Reading comprehension education in fifteen countries*. International Studies in Evaluation III. New York: Wiley.

Tyack, D., & Cuban, L. (1995). *Tinkering toward utopia: A century of public school reform*. Cambridge, MA: Harvard University Press.

Venezky, R. (1997). *Hearing on literacy: Why kids can't read*. Talk presented before the Committee on Education and the Workforce, United States House of Representatives, Washington, DC, July 10, 1997.

Venezky, R. (1998). *Reading instruction and reading research: What do we know and what should we do next?* Paper submitted to Pew Charitable Trusts and OERI, February 15.

Vygotsky, L. (1962). *Thought and language* (E. Hanfmann & G. Vakar, Eds. & Trans.). Cambridge, MA: MIT Press.

Walberg, H. J. (1990). Productive teaching and instruction: Assessing the knowledge base. *Phi Delta Kappan, 71,* 470–478.

Walberg, H. J. (1997). U.S. schools teach reading least productively. *Research in English, 30*(3), 328–434.

Walberg, H. J. (1998, November 4). Incentivized school standards work. *Education Week, 58*(10), 48–51.

Weber, G. (1971). *Inner-city children can be taught to read*. Washington, DC: Council for Basic Education.

Willms, D. (in press). Quality and inequality in children's literacy: The effects of families, schools and communities. To appear in *Developmental health: The wealth, of nations in the information age*.

Wilson, G. L. (1950). Arithmetic. In W. S. Monroe (Ed.), *The encyclopedia of educational research* (Rev. ed., pp. 44–57). New York: Macmillan.

Winerip, M. (1999, January 3). Homework bound. *Education Life* (supplement to *The New York Times*), pp. 28–31, 40.

Index

About the Author

Jeanne S. Chall, before her death in 1999, was an emeritus professor at Harvard University, Graduate School of Education, where she developed and directed the graduate program in reading, language, and learning disabilities and the Harvard Reading Laboratory. She wrote widely. Among her books are *Learning to Read: The Great Debate, Stages of Reading Development, Readability Revisited and the New Dale–Chall Readability Formula,* and *Qualitative Assessment of Text Difficulty.*

Dr. Chall was a member of the National Academy of Education and the Reading Hall of Fame, and served on the Board of Directors of the International Reading Association and the National Society for the Study of Education. She received many awards, including the Edward L. Thorndike award from the American Psychological Association for distinguished psychological contributions to education, the American Educational Research Association's award for significant contributions to educational research, and the Samuel T. Orton Award from the Orton Dyslexia Society.